# The Lightworker's Guide to Everyday Karma

By Tina Erwin, CDR USN (Ret)

Crystal Pointe Media Inc.,
San Diego, California

The Lightworker's Guide to Everyday Karma

A Karmic Savings and Loan Series Book

By Tina Erwin, CDR USN, Ret.

Published by Crystal Pointe Media, Inc.
San Diego, CA

ISBN 13: 9781732267343
ISBN 10: 1732267340
Copyright © 2011
2nd Edition 2018

All rights reserved. No part of this book may be reproduced or transmitted in any form or by any means, electronic or mechanical, including photocopying, recording, or by any information storage and retrieval system, without permission in writing from the author.
Tina@TinaErwin.com

### DISCLAIMER

The contents of this publication are intended for educational and informative use only. They are not to be considered directive nor as a guide to self-diagnosis or self-treatment. Before embarking on any therapeutic regimen, it is absolutely essential that you consult with and obtain the approval of your personal physician or health care provider.

Cover Design by Christine Fulcher

# Other Works

## Books
- The Lightworker's Guide to Healing Grief
- The Lightworker's Guide to Everyday Karma
- Ghost Stories from the Ghosts' Point of View, Trilogy
- Karma and Frequency
- Soul Evolution: Past Lives & Karmic Ties

## Podcast
- The Karmic Path Podcast: Available anywhere you listen to podcasts

## Knowledge Library
- On-Demand Spiritual and Metaphysical Classes found at: TheKarmicPath.com

# Dedication

This book is dedicated to all of those tireless and unsung Lightworkers everywhere who do the good work with rough hands and care-worn faces.

This book is dedicated to those infinitely patient ones who help when they are tired, fearful and uncertain.

This book honors the truly wonderful Lightworkers out there, whether rich, middle class and poor, who make the world work, and who always greet the world with the smiles that light all of our tomorrows. God Bless you, every one.

# Acknowledgments

I would like to gratefully acknowledge the support and critical input of my sister Andrea Harris, and her daughter Marisa, my daughter Jeanne Marie, my daughter-in-law Monica and my friend Laura Van Tyne.

I also appreciate the love and support of my husband Troy, and my children and their spouses: James and Amee, Andrew and Monica and Jeanne Marie and her husband Michael, and my brother-in-law Craig Harris.

I deeply appreciate the contributions of my brothers Paul and Pierre Debs and all of our friends and extended family.

I am deeply grateful to my teacher, Tashi Lightening.

I am sending a special thanks to my dear friends, Jackie Edwards, Diane Springer, Karen Ward, and Caryn Worcester.

# Table of Contents

Other Books by Tina Erwin......................................... vi

How to Use This Book: ................................................. 1

Introduction ................................................................. 2
   What is Karma? ............................................................ 2
   Historic Perception of Karma ..................................... 3
   What Is a Lightworker? ............................................... 5
   The Karmic Opportunity ............................................. 7

Week 1   What Did You Learn Last Year? ........... 8

Week 2   Pleasing Everyone ................................ 11

Week 3   Cancer ...................................................... 15

Week 4   Remembering Your Goodness, Life after Death .................................................................. 33

Week 5   The Ego of Arrogance .......................... 39

Week 6   If I Had It To Do Over . . . ..................... 44

Week 7   We Become Our Parents ..................... 49

Week 8   Spiritual Charades ................................ 54

Week 9   Look for the Reason ............................. 61

Week 10   Car Karma ............................................. 65

Week 11   Training Wheels .................................. 76

Week 12   Gratitude .............................................. 80

Week 13   The Darkness Within ........................ 84

Week 14   The Many Faces of Ego ..................... 87

Week 15   The Ego of Self-Importance ............ 90

Week 16   Questioning God ................................ 93

| | | |
|---|---|---|
| Week 17 | An Eye for an Eye | 97 |
| Week 18 | Compassion Fatigue | 100 |
| Week 19 | Maintaining the DNA Spiral: Intellectual/Emotional Factors, Specifically Friendships | 103 |
| Week 20 | The Spiritual Philosophy of What Constitutes a Perfect Mother | 107 |
| Week 21 | Flowers | 116 |
| Week 22 | Processing Catastrophic News: Creating Karmic Balance | 119 |
| Week 23 | The Ego of Self-Degradation: Poor Me! | 123 |
| Week 24 | Fathers | 127 |
| Week 25 | Parking Spaces | 132 |
| Week 26 | The Relentless Pursuit of Perfection | 136 |
| Week 27 | The Acceleration of Time | 140 |
| Week 28 | Why Don't Psychics Win the Lottery? | 144 |
| Week 29 | Friendship | 158 |
| Week 30 | Doing a Good Job | 161 |
| Week 31 | Psychic Addictions | 164 |
| Week 32 | The Nature of Forgiveness | 169 |
| Week 33 | The Brother of the Penitent Man | 182 |
| Week 34 | Karmic Challenges | 187 |

| | | |
|---|---|---|
| Week 35 | The Difference Between Enabling vs Empowering | 192 |
| Week 36 | Whatever You Want is OK … | 198 |
| Week 37 | Personal Power Presence | 202 |
| Week 38 | Post Traumatic Stress Disorder (PTSD) | 206 |
| Week 39 | Lightning Bugs | 218 |
| Week 40 | The Spiritual Path as Archeology | 221 |
| Week 41 | The Eyes of God | 226 |
| Week 42 | The Spiritual Closet of Body and Soul | 230 |
| Week 43 | The Fuel of the Universe | 234 |
| Week 44 | Cooking Karma | 238 |
| Week 45 | The Resonance of Fear | 241 |
| Week 46 | Karmic Time | 245 |
| Week 47 | How Do You Love Under Stress? | 249 |
| Week 48 | The Gift of Food is Love in Action | 256 |
| Week 49 | Giving and Receiving Gifts | 260 |
| Week 50 | Dropping into Drama | 265 |
| Week 51 | Christmas Time and Holiday Visits | 269 |
| Week 52 | The Birth of Christ | 273 |
| Bonus Week! | Mental Popcorn | 277 |
| Learn More About Tina and her Books | | 281 |

## How to Use This Book:

The best way to use this book is any way you want to use it!

You can open it up to any week and start reading.

You can begin at the beginning or begin at the end.

You can read one a week or one a day.

The best way is the way that works the best for you.

You may even find that you can just open it up and see if what you read answers a need that you are having at that moment. You just never know.

Everyday karma is all about the choices you make. See how the choices of what you choose to read, and when you choose to read it, affect you!

The Lightworker's Guide to

# Introduction

**What is Karma?**

Karma is a spiritual law of physics that states categorically that for every action there is an equal and opposite reaction. Karma is a law of the universe that applies to all living things, to all heavenly bodies, all planets and ultimately, to all beings.

Karma is the very nature of God's consciousness. Karma is the energy that propels all of us from one moment to the other and from one thought to the next. Karma has no beginning and no ending. Karma is the energy of the Divine that powers all that is. It is energy, which, by itself, is without definition. No one can define energy because energy is everything, never ending and never beginning yet ever being.

Karma is the supreme law of justice, the balance that holds all things together. Whether or not we believe that something is just or unjust, should or should not have happened, the perspective of a mortal soul pales in comparison to the laws of karma which are always just, always balanced and ultimately, always fair no matter what the situation, no matter how supreme the joy or how profound the sorrow.

The word karma itself is a Sanskrit term for action and reaction. Karma is also known as the law of consequences. The word karma literally means "action," and karma is both the power latent with actions and the results our actions bring. Looked at another way, karma means that whatever we do, with our bodies, speech, or minds, will have a corresponding result. This result is so sure, so predictable in its inevitability that the greater our study, the more humble is our awe and respect for how karma works. And even though we may not feel that we can always define karma, at least we can begin to understand that it is by the laws of karma that we are all eternally governed.

Ultimately, our actions and reactions act like a savings and loan. Sometimes our actions are savings put away so that we can have that money, or energy, returned to us at a future time. Other times, our questionable actions borrow against our good karmic bank accounts. All accounts are inevitably balanced. Every single positive karmic action will balance every single negative action. How we have used our savings will ultimately determine our spiritual path of soul evolution as we eternally seek our return ticket home to God.

## Historic Perception of Karma

All faiths have a belief in this concept and express it in some manner and all cultures have an understanding of the Law of Karma and we may know it by other names and phrases:

"Do unto others as you would have them do unto you."

"Whatever you do, comes back to you."
"What goes around comes around."
"As you sow, so shall ye reap."
"An eye for an eye."

The concept of an eye for an eye was a fundamental belief in the essence of this law. Unfortunately, many people took and applied that concept literally. This distortion of the law of karma became the cause for many devastating wars and, in an endless series of karmic reactions, resulting in ever more war.

Karmic action is not bound by time or space. The actions that balance another action can literally take millennia to resolve or reach balance. Put another way, the law of karma is eternally just, and that means that karma has eternity with which to work things out. This is why a person may not understand why a certain event takes place in this lifetime without rhyme or reason. That does not mean that the karmic wheel is not turning; it is. We just do not have a perspective on the operative event that created the reaction we are seeing in front of us.

But karma sees all events in the perspective of history because all history is recorded, every single moment we live and breathe. No energy spent in mortal life is ever karmically wasted. If we could just absorb this profound perspective, we could begin to have a greater handle on our day-to-day lives. Perhaps our frustrations would not seem so great, our tragedies so profound or our desires so important. Maybe if we could absorb an historical perspective, we could stop taking ourselves quite so seriously, laugh a bit more and even decide to be happy. Happy people make other people happy.

The greater level of happiness that is created around us, the more energetic interest we are creating in our karmic savings account. That positive interest/energy will always be returned to us in thousands of subtle positive ways. Irritable, angry selfish people borrow against their own historical savings account and end up getting a loan from the good graces of those around them. Sometimes the loan comes due. Then, whatever we have sown, we shall reap.

Is every difficult experience a karmic return on investment? Yes and no. Sometimes there are those interesting occasions when a soul wants specific experiences so that they can have an opportunity to handle them differently, to make different choices and to change his or her karmic path. This is the reason we have many lifetimes to work things out. The study of karma will take lifetimes to fully begin a basic understanding on the mundane level.

However, for the purposes of this book, each Karmic Savings and Loan chapter will provide a peek inside a facet of the jewel that is karma.

Included in these chapters are all kinds of day-to-day vignettes that arise, issues that we all are facing and challenges that seem extremely daunting. Each chapter will offer a karmic perspective on how to view a particular issue. Each chapter is simply a karmic perspective to ponder.

## What Is a Lightworker?

A Lightworker is a person who has come to understand the seen and the unseen world and realizes the need to fill both worlds with light. This is a person who observes, communicates and loves without judgment. This is a person who understands that all good deeds are Light Work and that this work is the real reason we are all here. What separates Lightworkers from other people who do good things is that Lightworkers are aware of their actions from a karmic perspective. They have taken responsibility for all that they do and they are acutely aware of the impact that his or her words and deeds have on others. They have an understanding of the karma they are creating, because it is a conscious choice.

Lightworkers see themselves as lighting the path, not just for themselves, but also for others. The concept of light is a clearing of the darkness that surrounds so many lives and it is an opening up of the heart and mind to the light of eternal love.

Lightworkers perform service in all kinds of seemingly insignificant ways, from cooking for their families, or taking care of families, keeping a car in excellent order, performing well at their job, even if it seems like mundane boring work. Lightworkers know that every task is important to someone and we all need people to be conscientious, every single day.

Lightworkers are human; they make mistakes, misjudge a situation and sometimes try too hard. Sometimes they take on guilt or become too arrogant about what they think is important for someone else to be doing. They are here for their experiences as well. No one is exempt from the experiences that life will offer all of us.

Perhaps the best way we can each become a Lightworker, is to do our very best each moment, appreciate each moment for the learning experience it is and always seek the highest good. This trio of actions will lift us up closer to the light of the Divine until we finally understand that living is only about seeking to bring the light of the Divine into every living moment. And finally, in each of these there will be a karmic opportunity all its own to understand.

## The Karmic Opportunity

The point of all of these Karmic Savings and Loan chapters is to offer us a way to look at life differently. Each day is a karmic opportunity if only we can see it that way. Each article will encourage us to look for the karmic opportunity that is the focus of each one. If we always look at adversity the same way, if we always respond in the same way, what will we have learned at the end of our lives? It would be sad to say that we learned very little.

But what if we could use these little philosophical gems to light our way? What if we could use this book as a tool to evaluate our own karmic path in a whole new light? At the end of each chapter there will be little karmic challenges we can use to see our day-to-day lives in a slightly different way. Maybe we can change our lives, or just change the way we respond to that nasty neighbor or difficult parent. Maybe we will look at our car differently, buy flowers for no reason and value the people we love a bit more.

Growth in each life is stubbornly measured by the way that we respond to each challenging scenario. Maybe we can respond slightly differently by using the new points of view provided here. Enjoy!

The Lightworker's Guide to

## Week 1   What Did You Learn Last Year?

No, this is not a test and no, papers will not be collected. This is just a rather good question for all of us to ponder.

Often we are encouraged to look to the New Year and just forget last year! Whew! That was a tough year glad that's over!!! No sense looking back, just focus on the future - - right?

Make those New Year's resolutions and try to stick to them, but hey, if you don't, what's the big deal? So you didn't keep your word to yourself, who will care? . . . and so on.

Yes, last year is history, your history, a history of your karmic record, so precious, so important that now is the time to review it. Each event in your life is an opportunity to grow and change for the better. Learn the lessons as they come up, but wait, first you have to recognize the lessons so that you do not repeat them. But what are lessons?

Look at this past year very seriously. Look at your relationships. Which ones grew, got significantly better and why? Which ones began to deteriorate and why?

What did you accomplish that you are proud of and what still needs to be done?

Perhaps a good way to do it is to go month by month and see how you did, just for yourself.

Now try this interesting exercise: look at the difficult situations with which you dealt. How did you do? If this same lesson or situation is presented to you again, how will you handle it? Karma keeps presenting the same lessons over and over until you finally get it, until you finally understand. The cycle of repeating the opportunity then stops, since you finally learned the lesson that was offered. Look back over the year and decide what lessons have ceased in your life, and are no longer being presented to you. This is a measure of emotional progress and that is something to be celebrated.

Notice if you are less angry, less emotional, more detached, yet at the same time more compassionate. Look at what you want to work on within yourself. Look for a new and an old you. Now decide how the old you would have handled something, and how the new you is choosing to handle things. Look for the differences.

If the holidays were difficult decide NOW, today, how they will be different next holiday season.

If you are choosing to do emotional work with someone, then make a list of what you want to work on. It is more effective to say that you want to work on these specific things than to just say: "I'm a mess..."

If you are working on improving your intuition, then review when you listened to your Higher Self and how it turned out. Likewise, review when you did not listen to your Higher Self and how it turned out. A very large part of soul evolution is learning to listen to your Higher Self on a consistent basis. Higher Self is that subtle voice that will guide you to the right karmic path if you choose to hear it.

This seems like a tall order. However, it is far more productive than making resolutions that you may never accomplish. Resolve to recognize the lessons and to learn from them. See you next year!

## The Karmic Opportunity

Now is the time to decide what you are willing to do to change how this year will be.

Look at keeping your word to yourself and others as a sacred oath.

Be sure to forgive yourself for the past.

Accept that each event is an experience and decide to embrace it for all of the powerful lessons it offers.

Start the New Year out by loving yourself.

## Affirmation

Every day is a wonderful new beginning.

## Week 2   Pleasing Everyone

One of the hardest things about being a loving, caring person, being a Lightworker, parent, spouse, child, friend, boss, employee or co-worker is that you just cannot please everyone.

Realizing that this is a pretty obvious statement is not necessarily helpful. However, it is good to look at how to handle the fact that some of the things you do and the decisions you make are going to be difficult, painful or hard for people.

Sometimes you simply have to make a decision and go with it. Sometimes you have to decide what is best for you in a given moment as well as evaluating how your actions are going to affect other people. Ultimately, you have to decide. Sometimes it is the indecision itself that becomes its own agony. It is easy to say, well, just make a decision and go with it. It is a lot harder to actually make that decision - to take that action.

There are unending examples. Having watched several people plan weddings, weddings alone are the classic scenario of how this will work. The bride must choose and make a million decisions. There is no way she will ever make all the parties in a wedding happy. It is not humanly possible. Someone's feelings are going to be hurt. Feel free to disagree only if you have never planned a wedding. Why does karma do this to you? Why can't we have one big happy family, or country or world?

Karma tests you in a myriad of ways so that you can know who you are and so that you can display courage and act on that courageous feeling. Without protagonists in any given situation, you could not grow and change, emerge and love. Look at the phenomena of any superhero. Without the bad guys, how would you ever know if the superhero is a true blue person? In storybooks, situations are good or bad. However in life, all things that are good just may not be good for you and therein lies the conundrum, the dilemma. In real life, white and black become a thousand shades of grey.

Now that you understand that no one can please everyone, how do you live in a world in which all of your decisions and karma are affected by how you influence other people, other places and other things?

Here are some modest suggestions. First of all, talk about it with someone you trust who has no overt agenda. Everyone has an agenda; a point of view and an understanding of how what you are talking about is going to influence him or her. It is the unique person who can separate him or herself, from the situation and be objective. These people exist but there are not many of them.

Look at the situation from everyone's view. If one person is unusually difficult or intimidating, decide how to approach that particular person so that he or she can believe that a positive feeling can come about from your decision. There are many ways to approach things but usually the shove-it-down-someone's-throat approach creates more enemies than taking a bit of extra time to figure out how to politically smooth the way.

Look at the worst-case scenario - in other words, what is the worst that can happen? Just how mad will someone get? We all seem to be terrified to see someone angry. Men freak out when women cry. Women often go to pieces when men start yelling. Well, people do get past anger and tears. They can get to the other side of it. If you are afraid of their actions, then go ahead and walk through the worst case scenario and then decide how you will feel and deal with it. You can handle it.

You can also ask for help in the room. You can ask for angels of peace and calming for both of you but you cannot ask for an angel to influence the other person. That is grey/black magic and it earns a darker degree of karma. However, asking for spiritual help to smooth the moment is allowed and encouraged.

Pick a date and time and just approach the subject. If the person gets angry, remain calm. You have already pre-lived their anger and you know that they will still be all right. Remember, the longer you wait to face a situation and take action, the worse and more difficult it becomes. Karma never lets you off the hook.

Do your best. That is all anyone can expect. Look at your actions with a clear conscience and do not allow guilt over the outcome to dissuade you. Sometimes you have to do what you have to do. When you are honest, things have a way of working out with grace.

## The Karmic Opportunity

Look back over past karmic opportunities and remember what worked well.

Look at what you did that was not politically correct but was karmically correct. A karmically correct answer will always carry the day.

Reach down inside yourself and find your moral courage.

Impose on your angels and ask for their help, delegate to them by requesting their help in bringing peace and calming to any situation.

Always focus on the greatest good for all concerned, not the easiest solution.

Request wisdom from your Higher Self and then take action.

## Affirmation

I believe in the strength of my decisions and my goodness as a person.

## Week 3  Cancer

### Peripheral Causes

There was an interesting article in a large city newspaper, which stated that diet did not make a big difference in whether or not someone's breast cancer returned. This seemed to baffle the doctors and the scientists of this study.

Does diet determine whether or not you are going to get cancer? No, it doesn't. Diet may contribute to setting up an environment where cancer can live, but what causes cancer is purely emotional. Cancer happens to a person for several reasons. Each has to do with experience: the experiences of mortal life.

Some peoples' mortal contract is at an end and it is time for them to leave. Often you will see an exceptionally aggressive cancer attack their body and they are literally gone within a week or a little more. He or she could have died in an accident or from an infection, or for some other reason. When your contract is over, you leave. There has to be a method for your departure and cancer is often the method that is used. Cancer offers its own unique set of experiences and that is why it happens to some people.

However, cancer that goes on for years and then the person survives or dies, has some very unique emotional causes. The emotional causes are often quite complicated. Cancer is not a solitary disease. It literally involves hundreds of caregivers and often all of someone's family members. The person with cancer calls himself or herself a victim, as if a crime were committed against him or her. The cancer 'victim' requires the attention of as many people as possible to get to the other side of the illness. It becomes an emotional roller coaster for all of the parties involved.

There is tremendous drama involved every day as the person goes through all the trials and physical anomalies of seeking to heal their cancer. They seem to have a tremendous need for the outpouring of love, compassion and attention their disease inspires. Once they seem to be on the other side of it, they still involve people with support groups, or cancer survivor meetings. They also wear ribbons - as a badge of some sort. The irony is that they never stop being a victim. Why? Because the 'emotional trauma' against them, that which is always unspoken, has never been healed and until you heal the underlying 'emotional trauma', you can only marginally hope to heal cancer.

Whatever the initiating traumatic event that so deeply affected this person was, that event still needs attention. Also, profound grief and/or multiple grief events can have a similar effect on a person's body. The emotional part of that person may desperately need some form of attention to heal and cancer offers them this outpouring of loving attention.

People also say that they 'got cancer - as if it is something someone has given them and now they 'have' it. No one ever says that they caught it, got infected with it, picked it up, or came down with it. The reason is that each person with cancer has literally infected himself or herself with cancer because it specifically develops from inside of them.

What causes cancer is basically a math problem with an emotional twist. Our cells have an operating frequency. When the frequency of our cells drops below a certain number, we are now in a position to allow cancer to be triggered by our bodies, if we need it, if we need that experience.

'If we need it.' Why would anyone need cancer? Why does having cancer satisfy a need in anyone? Cancer very often satisfies a tremendous need for attention in an astounding number of people. As the need for attention, care, compassion and love grows, often, so also grows his or her cancer until neither the need nor the cancer can be ignored. It just hurts so much inside that the person has to do something about it. Replace the word 'hurt', with the words 'emotional trauma'. When the pain of the person's 'emotional trauma' becomes so great, their body decides to get his or her attention and frequently that attention getter, is cancer.

What is 'emotional trauma?' 'Emotional trauma' is an event or series of events in a person's life that has a huge impact on that person at the cellular level. It is almost as if the echo of that trauma, the profound nature of that trauma causes a change in the person's cells. What types of trauma might these be? The death of a close family member, such as a parent, sibling, close grandparent, close friend causes profound grief. Very often that grief is not healed. Another type of serious trauma is sexual abuse of any kind by anyone from a parent or sibling to a trusted clergyman or teacher. The violation of trust in a safe world creates a shadow of fear in a person, which that individual may never be aware of on a conscious level. The event very probably happened so that the person could learn how to heal their life, but few people come to understand this at this level of insight. Often the traumatic event is tossed off as not that big a deal, or worse the person loses all memory of the event. Sometimes, the trauma is so impossible for a child or adult to deal with that they suppress it completely, as if it never happened.

In a situation where the traumatic event is suppressed, the person often cannot begin to identify what the 'emotional trauma' is, or they have been denying it for so long, that they cannot now bring it to consciousness. Since they cannot either identify the 'emotional trauma' or work through it if they have actually identified it, the body says, well, we have to do something to heal our wounded hearts, so let us do this cancer thing to receive some loving attention.

Literally, cancer is an emotional hurt or emotional need that has never been adequately answered with love and care. When someone has cancer they generally receive a lot of desperately needed loving attention.

Listen to a person with cancer talk about all the attention they are receiving. Some will say that their marriage improved, or their children were more attentive or their neighbors helped them or they met all these wonderful people on the Internet who were there for them. All of a sudden, they are not alone. They are also receiving focused, often daily attention from their doctors, hospital staff, clinics, support groups, and other people. Perhaps in the past the person did not know how to ask for help, but cancer gives them a socially acceptable method for legitimately receiving this desperately needed help.

The need for attention is also a need for energy. When we are in deep despair, we seldom have enough energy to power our days. If we feel emotionally powerless, we lack energy on so many levels. When we have cancer, we have a legitimate reason for people to give us their love and energy and we can feel justified in taking it when it is so generously offered. However, if we are not sick, we may not feel that we can reach out and ask for help. We may not feel deserving of anyone's attention.

There is another aspect here. If a person has given everyone else his or her energy for a very long time, but never felt that that energy was returned, a sense of resentment may have grown, physically and emotionally. If there is no way to dissipate this irritating feeling, the body will just absorb it until eventually the body says enough! It has to be my turn, and the negative energy of the anger/resentment, 'emotional trauma' or profound sadness, has to manifest. Then when people shower this person with their loving energy, they finally feel that they are seeing a return on previously spent energy.

## Potential Cancer Initiators

What is this need for attention? Where does it come from? Let us now open up our compassionate hearts and look at the types of cancer and the types of 'emotional traumas' that set these illnesses in motion.

Incest takes place in an astounding number of families. It is the unspoken terrible crime that affects men and women. The person often feels dirty, ashamed and many suffer from a feeling of somehow being punished. The reproductive and breast/chest areas are never fully, if ever, loved. If you do not love your body, all the parts of it, you are forever out of balance. The following types of cancer may manifest from incest: uterine, pancreatic, cervical, colon, prostate, lung, rectal, and breast cancer.

Rape of both men and women is a staggering 'emotional trauma', one that affects a person all of his or her life. The person suffers not only the initial trauma, but also long term post traumatic stress syndrome. It is such a terribly ugly 'emotional trauma.' People want you to just 'get over it' so it will not be in their faces. Rape by clergymen is the most heinous, criminal 'emotional trauma' because it totally separates the person from God. The person feels so out of balance that they cannot find their way back. Since there is no real healing without God, how is a person supposed to heal from the damage caused by a priest or clergyman? The following types of cancer may manifest from rape: uterine, pancreatic, cervical, colon, lung, breast cancer, skin, and bone - all types can come from this most intimate crime.

Abortion is another 'emotional trauma', which, if not properly grieved, atoned for and healed, may set the person up for cancer. The emotional trauma in this situation is whatever caused the woman to be in that situation in the first place. On the other hand, women who give their children up for adoption also suffer terribly, but they also feel that they were giving their children a better life than they could have personally given them. There is a different feeling associated with that action. Again, all types of cancer may come from the abortion situation.

Abuse of any kind, whether it is physical, mental, emotional, or spiritual, can take a person to levels of tremendous despair and create within them, a sense of aloneness. It does not have to be physical abuse, to create 'emotional trauma'. Some people are so devastated by the lack of love in their lives, or of feeling unwanted, that the need to find it often leads them down the cancer road. It doesn't have to, but for some people, it does.

Grief, a deep, intimate and heart crushing emotion, can also lay the seeds for various types of cancer, specifically lung, colon and breast cancer. The loss of the love of your life, the loss of a child or the loss through death, divorce or abandonment of a parent may be so devastating that the individual has a very difficult time recovering emotionally. This keeps the body out of balance, sometimes, for most of a person's life. Grief, like other traumas can be healed but much emotional/spiritual work is required to get a person to a more balanced level.

Profound sadness from multiple scenarios may create a cancerous environment - a grief unhealed, or a love that is lost - whatever is the cause of the sadness, can act like the emotional trigger to allow the person to self-generate cancer.

## Paths to Healing Cancer

What heals that part of us that has suffered from any type of 'emotional trauma' or profound sadness? There are, alas, no easy answers. Whatever has happened to us has happened for a reason, and that reason is to teach us all kinds of spiritual lessons. Sometimes, those lessons are very, very difficult. We often find that we profoundly resent the fact that we have to deal with these traumas.

No one has an easy life, despite how television may make it seem. Each one of us comes here for profound lessons. The faster we learn these lessons, the faster we evolve as souls.

So, the question before us is how do we heal a body that now has active cancer?

And the response is: What are we willing to do to heal?

People will go through tortuous procedures and drugs that decimate the body and reduce it to a terrible and often hairless place. They will allow body parts to be lopped off, removed or cut out. Sometimes, surgery is vital to stop the spread. There is often no question that this has to be done. However, many may find it far more tortuous to look at the emotional causes of their cancer. They hate the mutilation to their bodies and vow to fight until the end! Wow, fighting really takes a lot of emotional, mental and spiritual energy. So, what if you could look at your body very, very differently?

What if you stopped fighting cancer and embraced your body? What if you stopped fighting yourself, punishing yourself for whatever took place earlier in your life? Could you then use more holistic techniques and begin to work with the very concepts of how you view yourself and begin to heal yourself emotionally at the cellular level?

When you stop fighting your body and learn to love your body, you readily embark on that journey of healing your body. If you do not know what you are healing, if you think it is a tumor or cancer spot, then you miss the lesson of why you have the illness in the first place. The cancer is the messenger that something is wrong with the emotional body. The tragedy is that when you fight the messenger with all of your being, you seldom get the real message you need to learn from the experience.

The emotional body is a facet of our personality that houses our feelings about ourselves. All kinds of things influence this emotional body, every life experience, all the verbal cues we are given that help us to understand who we are affect and form our emotional body. Consider how an individual is harmed by being told that he or she 'was born in sin and will die in sin and that this person will have to face all of their terrible misdeeds on judgment day!' Can you imagine how incredibly detrimental these statements could be for anyone? It means that no matter what you have done that is good in your life, it will not matter on 'judgment day!'

Consider this example: a woman is flying on an airplane and several passengers engage her in a discussion of religion. All of a sudden, the man behind her pipes up that he is a terrible person, that he has done terrible things and that there is no way that God can ever forgive him. He notes that his religion has already informed him that he is going to hell. He is never given any hope and at the tender age of 18 believes that the rest of his life he is supposed to be punished. None of the listening passengers could believe what he was saying and no one on that plane ever knew what that young man had done, but just perhaps each of them silently hoped that God would in fact forgive him. In this actual example, this young man is being set up for cancer through the very powerful impetus of guilt. The more guilt, the worse the emotional body of any person is going to feel. The bottom line here is that guilt always seeks punishment and cancer is a very, very powerful punishment. Guilt drops the physical frequency of the emotional body. The lower the frequency of any person's body, the harder it is for that person's body to ward off any type of illness from a cold to cancer.

Understanding the scenario above is important, because one of the critical challenges here is to get past the cancer diagnosis. The word cancer itself strikes fear in the hearts of even the most courageous souls. Perhaps the first step is not to be intimidated by the diagnosis. Then we can begin to move toward the next steps.

The key is to begin to understand what causes the frequency of the body to drop to such a low level and to bring it back up to a much higher level. The point is to embrace the journey that enables us to unlock the places in our hearts that are dark, guilty or hurting and open them up to spiritual/emotional healing.

There is no healing the physical/mental body without connecting the emotional/spiritual body to the Divine. There is no deep, emotional healing without feeling that, at the level of the Divine, we are loved by God and that we can use that Divine love to heal all the parts of us that need healing.

The cancer is eating away at the physical/mental body. We must ask ourselves what is eating us emotionally and spiritually. Never discount the event, or accumulation of events that happen because the sum of those events absolutely contributes to where we each are at this moment.

One of the most profound questions we can ask ourselves is how much do we love? Not just surface love but such a deep love that it runs to the very core of us. Do we love anything or anyone, with all of our hearts?

Many people find that when they are 'in love' or love what they do and whom they are with, they are not 'in pain'. If an 'emotional trauma' or profound grief happened to us, we may feel that we can never trust being 'in love' or loving again. Many people feel that they cannot trust love; they can only trust pain. Some people believe that they only know that pain is real and reliable. Mental and emotional pain can take us to such a dark place. How do we find the courage to take that scary step and find the path to being 'in love/loving' again?

What causes us to feel that we are out of love? If someone betrays us who is supposed to love us or be true to us, it causes us to be afraid to love completely. This 'betrayer' can be a spouse, parent or other family member, a trusted friend of the family, a clergyman or a teacher. If this person also perpetrated an 'emotional trauma,' we may never feel that we can trust again. Without trust, we feel vulnerable and we may be filled with despair and that despair will literally eat away at our bodies. Cancer can eat at us for a long period of time or it can come suddenly and literally destroy us quickly.

Whatever the events that may have happened to us, that marched us down the road of victimhood or grief also robbed us of our sense of power. If we feel powerless and out of love, how do we continue to grow and mature emotionally? We are either busy living or we are busy dying. We have to decide what will, in the end, define us.

## Thriving After Cancer

If a person has tremendous depth of insight and is willing to do whatever it takes to heal for as long as it takes to heal, this person will find that once the journey is embraced, he or she can begin to learn all about how to find that place where they can be 'in love' and love again. We have to reverse the effect of the 'emotional trauma,' resentment or grief. And while no one can do this for us, we may find, however, that when we are ready for this journey, a teacher will appear to help us.

We will have to become a detective and be willing to look in all those emotionally dark places to collect the clues, to find the answers and to solve the puzzle. We have to stop punishing ourselves for whatever happened and leave the emotional prison of victimhood. We have to forgive the criminal act or trauma, and we can only do that by embracing the often exceptionally painful lessons offered. Forgiving the act does not mean that what was done is acceptable. It means that we embrace the lesson and use the key that is forgiveness to unlock our emotional prison and allow ourselves to be set free. As long as we are in that emotional prison, the other person or the situation continues to have power over us. When we take our power back, we heal ourselves. We may also have to face removing a toxic person from our lives and we may have to be willing to make some critically, fundamental changes.

When we heal ourselves, we are now free, really free. We can finally be free to love again and to trust again. Nothing is eating away at us.

One other critical element is to be grateful to the very body that was eating away at itself for the message it was desperately trying to tell us. Pain and anomalies in the body are messages from the subconscious that something is terribly wrong. When we keep ignoring the messages and deny the existence of the messenger, the messenger has to knock at the door harder and louder until finally we get the message.

Once we finally get the message, we have to embrace the messenger and that messenger is our body. Love this body. We must stop being at war with our body. Stop fighting the cancer and love the cancer message of healing that can be conveyed. Thank the body for providing this message, this experience of growth, insight and understanding. Reward this body with loving kindness and care. Vow never to use an unkind word toward this body again. Loving the body is a powerful act of healing.

There are many people for whom cancer is just an old but precious memory. They find that they are grateful to their bodies for the lesson of the cancer. Without the cancer, they would not have discovered the amazing path to healing. They might never have learned how many people loved them either. Some people have repaired their marriages. Some have discovered what is really important to them in their lives.

Eventually what they find is life itself. They find that they do love the body that may have been violated, hurt, beaten or verbally belittled. They solved the emotional trauma and stopped being a victim. They also stopped being a survivor.

Survivors endlessly hang on, hoping to survive each day; they are barely there. People who are really living are thriving.

If we are 'in love' with life, we are capable of thriving in all we do. The hope for those who love life is that eventually, everyone will come to love all that life has to offer, the good and the unsavory messages as well as the messengers. Once we can do that, we can become a powerfully loving and thriving human being. Once we can see ourselves as that kind of a person, we will never need cancer in our lives again. We will have changed our resonance. And speaking of resonance, beware the very dangerous resonance of pink.

## The Dangerous Resonance of Pink

Resonance is a critically important metaphysical concept to understand. Everything has a frequency. Resonance is the concept that you resonate, or are in harmony with something, someone, some place or with some concept that is the same frequency as yours, or is close to that frequency.

When you resonate with something, you take on those characteristics because you agree with what it is saying. So, it is exceptionally important to pay attention to all those things in which you are in resonance.

You have to consciously decide, and choose with what you will be in resonance. However, what if you are not aware that somehow you are becoming in resonance with a concept that could be exceptionally harmful to you? Could this happen? Is it possible?

It is possible and it is happening right before your eyes. Women today are being made to believe on an exceptionally subtle level that they will inevitably get breast cancer. At some point, there is a subtle pressure to believe that no matter what you do, this terrible thing is going to happen to you. Some women are so afraid of this that they are going ahead and having whole body parts removed in advance. They are allowing themselves to be mutilated to preclude breast cancer. American women are becoming completely in resonance with breast cancer.

How is this resonance being perpetrated? Pink! Wear pink for the Cure! There is Breast Cancer Awareness Week, Month, Year, Day, Sale, Offer, and on and on. At first it started out with pink bracelets, and then pink ribbons. Now everywhere you look, you see this toxic manipulation of your psyche through the most astounding things such as selling pink kitchen appliances, pink computer/phone technologies, Fight For the Cure jewelry - which you wear in the vicinity of your breasts - of course.

There are also marathons. "Race for the Cure!!!" they say. Imagine hundreds of women running a marathon, all in resonance with each other and all thinking about breast cancer. All mistakenly thinking their running is going to somehow stop what they now believe in the recesses of their minds is inevitable: breast cancer.

Some soup now comes in cans with pink labels, so eat the soup and think of breast cancer.

Carpet companies give discounts if you buy 'pink flooring' and they will donate to 'the cure for breast cancer.'

One bakery in Virginia even sells bagels in the breast cancer ribbon shape and wraps them in pink paper.

And the absolute worst pink product: breast cancer awareness underwear in pink bras and panties. Think about it. You are being asked to wear the representation of breast cancer directly on your very breasts. So even as you get dressed, you are putting on a pink bra that will cradle the very breasts that just may have to be removed.

That is a lot of fear. That is a tremendous number of women to place in fear and to place this fear in front of them day after day, week after week, and year after year. The drug companies are literally creating the very market they are telling people they want to eliminate - breast cancer patients. But breast cancer is very, very big business. Breast cancer advertising is an even bigger business on very subtle levels.

Over the past seventy years, billions of dollars have been donated to find a cure. Where is this money from all of these fund raising activities actually going? Where is the cure for cancer?

This resonance issue goes a step further. Not only are you being made to be afraid of your very bodies, you are being made to believe that fighting your body will somehow keep you safe.

There are now millions of extremely sincere, conscientious women, in resonance with each other, wearing an insipid shade of pink thinking that they are standing side by side with other women of like mind who want to find a cure for a disease they do not even have but believe that they will probably, eventually get. There is no logic here, only exceptionally brilliant advertising. You surely don't see men wearing shiny brown ribbons to fight prostate or testicular cancer. You absolutely don't see men having their prostates removed or testicles lopped off - just in case. No man in his right mind would do such an illogical thing.

These resonance issues also apply to women who have already had breast cancer. By keeping them in resonance with breast cancer, they stay labeled 'breast cancer survivors' forever. When do they heal? When is it over? When do the support groups end?

People who wear these bracelets and pins think they are being supportive, but potentially, they could be harming themselves.

So, what can you do to change your resonance? Look at the following positive, exceptionally inexpensive karmic opportunities to keep yourself happy, healthy and potentially forever cancer free. The time has come to shift your resonance to being with people who are happy, healthy and who are enjoying the life and the body they have. Now is the time to become in resonance with a whole new wonderful reality and enjoy a healthy life for the rest of your life.

# The Karmic Opportunity

Always look for the underlying emotional cause of cancer.

Seek to heal your own emotions and cancer may never develop in your body.

Decide that you will never need the experience of cancer.

If you already have or have had cancer decide that you are learning the lessons that cancer offers and that you can cease its affect on your body. You can decide this. Accept the power that this opportunity offers you.

If you are in need of extra love and attention, go ahead and ask for it. Tell your friends and family that you do have an ache in your heart and you need their help in healing it. You can also seek outside professional help.

If you have awareness of your private trauma or suffering give yourself permission to talk about it and to heal it. Do not wait for your body to tell you that there is a problem.

Seek the reason any experience has happened and embrace that experience for the lessons it is offering. Open your mind to the possibility of tremendous growth.

Ask for Divine intervention to heal you, even if you already have cancer.

Love with all of your heart. Always be in love.

When you are ready to begin your spiritual journey of growth, a teacher will appear. Start looking for this teacher.

Love your body and love the experiences you have been blessed with, even the most difficult ones. Gratitude raises your frequency.

Strike the word 'survivor' from your vocabulary. Survivors are just barely hanging on. Decide to be a thriving personality, healthy and happy.

Boycott all pink breast cancer products! Be politically incorrect!

Do not allow advertising to create fear in you. Demand an accounting of where this money is going and stop donating to the drug companies.

Love your body!

Be grateful to your body for its long-standing service to you.

Anoint your beautiful body with essential oils. Dress your beautiful body in clothes that make you feel like a million dollars. Get a hair and fashion makeover if necessary to see a new you!

Wear colors that make you happy.

Make peace with your body and give it the love and respect that it truly deserves. Be grateful for the body you have, no matter what its shape.

Live and be happy. Say good-bye to the breast cancer cause.

Shift your resonance to being healthy.

Consciously choose that with which you will be in resonance.

Love life, love living.

## Affirmations

Day by day in every way my body is getting stronger, healthier and happier.

I love every amazing facet of my body, every day.

I always have access to divine power to heal my body.

## Week 4    Remembering Your Goodness, Life after Death

How you view yourself in life is exactly how you are going to view yourself in death. If you believe yourself to be a good person in life, then when you die, you are very likely to believe that you are worthy of moving into the light. Souls who do not see themselves as worthy of God's love, will not move toward the light when they are no longer attached to a physical body.

One of the most curious things for any medium to see is the disembodied soul who is haunting a friend, relative or a location. What is so baffling is that this can happen to people who spent their whole lives going to church. Their families may have seen them as profoundly devout people, going to church, synagogue, or temple religiously, every week, perhaps teaching Sunday school and helping out in church activities. However, once they have left the physical body, they do not move into the light.

Why? Surely, these are the people who would welcome the opportunity to be closer to God. Unfortunately, being heavily involved in any specific religion does not necessarily bring a person closer to God. Church may make it seem more convenient, but a connection to the Divine has to live within you; you cannot find it in any building of wood and stone.

When a medium asks the soul why he or she has not moved on, routinely, the person will say that they did not lead a good enough life when they were in a mortal body. Some will say that they are not worthy. Others will say that they did something that they "are not proud of" at some point in his or her life and that for this act, they can never be forgiven. They will tell you that they will never be worthy 'enough.' Others will remind you of their church teaching that says that they were born in sin and that they will die in sin and that they are never going to be worthy enough for Christ's sacrifice. Some will say that once a sinner, always a sinner and on and on. The church dogma literally haunts the soul long after death.

So, just how worthy does any soul have to be to move into the light? Even after death, souls have free will and that free will even extends to the choice each soul makes when they literally "walk through the valley of the shadow of death." Even though they may have recited the 23rd psalm a thousand times in life, it does not mean that they believe it to be true for themselves in death.

Believe in yourself. Believe in God, no matter what religious label you place upon Him. At the end of a life, you are just as dead whether you are Christian, Muslim, Buddhist, Hindu or Jewish. Death is no respecter of religion. Every single soul has to pass through the fourth dimension before entering the dimensions of the Heaven World or the lower astral. For each soul who believes him or herself to be a good person, the passage is relatively uneventful, quick and positive. For others, the journey is endless and can take them to some quite distasteful places. What this means is that if you believe that you are not worthy, you create

## Everyday Karma

for yourself a place of greater or lesser degrees of spiritual punishment. What might this be like? Sometimes, the soul does not feel released from physical pain. In another case the soul may still see the apparitions that haunted them in life still haunting them in death. Some believe that their sense of worthlessness will punish them by being in a cold, dark place – and the list continues. Consider the following example.

There was once a very religious grandmother who died and did not feel worthy of the light of heaven and ended up in the lower astral plane. She thought she was to be punished because she did not believe she was a very good parent, grandparent and person, even though her family loved her. When the medium asked her why she felt this way, she said that she thought she was being humble to believe this about herself and she also felt that she was, after all, a sinner. She was quite grateful to learn that no matter what she thought she had done, that she would always be welcomed home by God. This case ended well for this dear grandmother who was provided with a glorious Angel of Transition to guide her to the correct realm of the heaven world.

In another case, a man who had committed suicide kept haunting his wife because he was so sorry for taking his own life and causing her such pain. He did not realize that by haunting her, he was literally terrifying her. The medium who helped him, asked him if he had seen the light, which in fact, he had. He did not go into it because he felt that he was not a good person, exacerbated by the act of killing himself. He was quite relieved to know that he could be welcomed into the light and, as he made that transition, his grandmother met him.

In another example, a man who never gave any thought to the spiritual side of life died suddenly in an accident and to his intense surprise, found himself standing, actually hovering, outside of his body. All he could think of was how upset his wife would be that he wrecked their brand new car. Eventually, he found himself quite bewildered. He had no idea what to do now that he was actually no longer in that body. Even when the light came, he felt guilty and did not move toward what he felt was comforting light. He did receive assistance and he did eventually move on. However, imagine how much less spiritual stress he would have endured, if he had understood what happens at death and that help was available to him.

Some people are just dumbfounded to discover that once the physical body is no longer able to be used, that they just keep on living in a different dimension. In truth, they literally never miss an energetic beat and find life outside of their body very natural although confusing at first. Then they begin to remember all of the deeds they did in mortal life, the good, the bad and the ugly ones. They know they are supposed to do something, but are baffled as to how to proceed next.

Most religions counsel a person while alive. Few advise them of the steps to take once they have left the body. Where do they think the energy of life goes once the physical body dies? That is the time that a personality needs a lot of guidance! So, once you leave the body, ask God to forgive you for your deeds during this most recent mortal life. Then ask for Divine assistance, and/or angels or just ask God to help you find your way home. Remember, you can ask for Angels of Transition to help you and perhaps others who may have died with you. You can also request the assistance of Jesus, Buddha, Sri

Krishna or any of the great ones who have helped us throughout time.

That is the key. No matter what you may think of yourself, the opportunity for heavenly counsel is open to you. What you believe to be true about yourself colors your path of mortal and non-mortal existence, for eternity. It is always important to remember to love yourself.

Understanding death is important. Removing the fear of the process of death is utterly critical for everyone. Learning how to help yourself and possibly others is very powerful indeed. The light will come automatically most of the time. When it arrives, move toward it, no matter how you feel about yourself. Trust that this is the Divine way. Trust that you will be all right, and that those whom you have left behind will also be all right. Look forward to being welcomed home by someone you recognize. And finally, look forward to the powerful opportunity to review your life, no matter what happened in that life. The Great Ones are always there to help you gain insight and understanding. God loves every one of us, no matter who we are or what we have done.

## The Karmic Opportunity

Remember your goodness, even on difficult days. This raises your frequency.

Remember that God loves you no matter what you have done or what has happened in your life.

Remember that you are forgivable.

## Affirmation

## The Lightworker's Guide to

I am filled with the power, protection, love and blessings of Almighty God.

## Week 5   The Ego of Arrogance

When we think of ego and arrogance, many dictators come to mind, such as Napoleon, Hitler or Castro. We are so glad that we are not like them! Well, in their situations, it is obviously arrogance taken to a staggering level. How do we recognize and understand arrogance in day-to-day life? What does it look like?

Arrogance can be the father who will not listen to his teenage son who has a better idea, because the father does not realize that he is in competition with or is jealous of his son. The same is true of the mother who is such a great cook but will not teach her children to cook lest they become a better cook than she is or many other reasons.

Arrogance is the doctor who believes he/she knows it all and does not ask for a consult, or will not listen to the patient or, more critically, the nurse trying to point out something that could save a life.

Arrogance is the military officer who is so full of his or her own importance that he or she will not listen to the junior enlisted person who may actually have the answer to the situation. Lives will be lost in combat or in day-to-day equipment maintenance hazards because of this level of arrogance.

# The Lightworker's Guide to

Arrogance is the insecure boss who wants to take all the credit and is afraid that other creative employees will be promoted over him or her.

Arrogance is a form of fear, an insecurity that means that what a person has is not enough, that something inside them is not good enough or capable enough. A really secure person knows who they are and what they know. They also know how to surround themselves with really smart people who can work as team members. It is terrific to be the leader, but it is also a wonderful feeling to be part of a team that is working together for a common goal.

Arrogance is the fear of admitting that you do not have all the answers, but pretending that you do.

Arrogance is jealousy that there will not be enough for you, so you take what you smugly think is rightfully yours -- but is it?

Arrogance is the ego of never admitting a mistake or never saying you are sorry for the hurt you may have caused.

Arrogance is sabotaging someone else by deciding that the end justifies the means when it just does not.

Arrogance is the person who views him or herself as so important that they believe that they are above the law. This includes elected officials of all parties, clergymen, military people, teachers, movie stars, government officials, Congress, and police, to name a few. When you operate at that level of power, karma offers you a rare opportunity to do the right thing by making honest and karmically significant, often selfless, contributions.

Arrogance is desperately seeking to control everyone and everything around you. This impossible

# Everyday Karma

goal of total control is why so many arrogant people are intensely disliked.

Arrogance is believing in all of the press that says that you are famous and believing that everyone wants to hear your opinion now that you are famous.

A secure person knows what they do not know and who to ask to get the answer.

A secure person realizes that you never really control anything, allowing for the natural flow.

A secure person can make a mistake and be readily forgiven, because they can say that they screwed up and that they are sorry; it only takes a moment. The arrogant person simply cannot admit their mistakes and consequently they often find that people will look for their mistakes.

A secure person senses immediately that something is not right and asks for the answer, asks if they have made a mistake and listens to see if there is more to learn.

A secure person is humble, willingly offering credit to the originator of a thought, idea, invention or plan. By showcasing the other person, what they frequently receive in return is gratitude, which empowers teamwork. A good leader in combat, an operating room or a boardroom is the one person who has not the larger view, but the very largest perspective. This person also has the ability to communicate that view to the entire team, even if that team is 100,000 people strong.

Examples of people working hard, but not arrogant who made/make a difference:

Mr. Fred Rogers [Mr. Rogers of children's television fame] – He was humble and loving to his last breath.

# The Lightworker's Guide to

Mother Theresa – She was so humble that she chose to slip away as the media focus was on Princess Diana's death.

Neale Donald Walsh - Works on encouraging everyone to talk to God, keeping the focus on the work, not himself.

Colonel Sanders – Another person so humble that he would pop in on any franchise restaurant and go right in and begin cooking. He also used his wealth to send many, many kids on a full scholarship to college.

President George Washington defined humility when he decided on his 'title' after being elected to lead this new country. He chose Mr. Washington, President of the United States rather than 'Your Highness,' 'Emperor' or 'King.' Washington understood that when he was no longer President he would return to who he had always been, a gentleman farmer. He realized that his time as General Washington and President Washington were merely temporary titles, worn when needed, and then humbly and rightly set aside. At the end of the day, at the end of his life, he still saw himself as an ordinary man, living in extraordinary times.

One of the best role models of the recent past was the Captain Kirk, Star Trek character. In this character, you get to see how personal power coupled with controlled ego enabled our hero to explore the Universe or at least his section of the quadrant to which he was assigned. Leading by example is challenging, but then if you expect to soar in the stars, you have to embody the very essence of controlled ego, humility and a profound belief in yourself. In this fictional character, the balance between having the confidence to face the vast unknown was coupled with the elegant ability to build a powerful team where everyone's contribution was critically important.

The bosses, parents, teachers, and friends who are enhanced by the success of those around them, their kids, students and friends, are the classic examples of secure people. These people know that the growth and progress of another is the growth and progress of us all, because we are all connected. So, let us ponder those we know who are humble and successful all at the same time and let them be our role models.

## The Karmic Opportunity

Remember that the success of the one is the success of the whole.

The generosity with which you share credit is directly proportional to the credit that is shared with you.

Karma always balances poor leadership in some way.

Believe in the people around you and they will reward you in a thousand ways.

Be the team player everyone wants on his or her team.

## Affirmation

The strength of my ego is always used as the light for others and to see the goodness in other people.

The Lightworker's Guide to

## Week 6  If I Had It To Do Over . . .

"If I had it to do over, surely I would do things differently," we hear people say. Well, the truth is that we do have it to do over, and over and over. That is the very essence of reincarnation: the opportunity to do it differently the next time.
Karma is always fair, just and timely. When we need an experience, it is offered to us. What creates the need for a specific experience is the reality that the last time we were presented with various options, perhaps we chose poorly. Karma gives us the opportunity to do it over with courage and wisdom the next time.
What things do we need to learn? The obvious ones are how we react to people, how we handle difficult situations and a test of our ethics and moral standards as well. Wisdom only comes from the experiences we analyze, take responsibility for and decide that, when next presented, we will react differently.
Let's go behind the cosmic scenes for a moment and look at the karmic mechanism. Take this life example: you live a life with a difficult person. You respond in specific ways. The person is never pleased. You are chronically filled with despair. You live a life where you give all your power to that person, trying to

# Everyday Karma

please him or her. You never find the courage to stand up to this person. You die. You move into the heaven world. The wonderful and wise beings that meet you offer you the opportunity to see how your life worked out from a cosmic perspective. You can see how your actions helped or hurt people and how you hurt or helped yourself. You are shown how you reacted to that person and how your reactions perpetuated your own despair. Finally, you feel that you understand. Ah, you say, next time I will do it differently, I just know it. So, you get to do it all over again.

The question that we always ask is if we were able to understand it so clearly in the heaven world, why do we not remember it when we reincarnate? Why do we seemingly make the same mistake over and over? Excellent question! And the answer is that karma just does not work that way. Think of the statement: If I had it to do over again, I would surely do it differently. Well, karma is setting you up to do just that but there is a catch.

The catch is that you have to start with exactly the same karmic parameters, otherwise you will not learn. A few rare people actually do remember the information they were provided in the heaven world. They do react with greater wisdom. However, for the rest of us, once the veil of forgetfulness comes upon us at birth, the conscious memory of what we learned in the heaven world is not available to us. Karma does this deliberately so that we can have the supreme opportunity to do it again and either react in the same way, or to do it differently: truly, the essence of free will. Karma puts us right where we started to go off course the last time. Usually, that is being born into the same family, with literally the same family members so that we can have the opportunity to learn these lessons again. While we may not necessarily have the same exact role in that family life after life, we do get to have those variations on a theme, which enable us to learn.

Returning to our example, you are again born into a family with a parent who cannot be pleased. You instinctively return to the pattern of trying to please that person. It does not work for, say, the first 40 years of your life. Then one day you pray for an answer and you read something that helps you to understand that in the next 1000 years you will never please this person. Why are you giving your power away to them? Why? Who is it serving? However, since this person is a parent, you are caught in the 'parent trap' of trying to be a conscientious good son or daughter, which explains your efforts to please them.

You decide to muster up the courage to not care whether you please them. Finally, you decide to live your life and do the right thing for yourself. Your family complains that you are a bad person. Still, you maintain your courage and begin to separate from this demanding, energy-draining, manipulating parent. You begin to pull away.

What karma does next is very interesting. Karma always wants to know if you really learned the lesson. So, you may find that similar personality types are placed in your path to see if your courage was a one-time thing, or does this understanding that you are not responsible for the happiness of another person really live within you? If it does then you will have passed an important cosmic milestone; you will not need to repeat this lesson.

Now, different people will appear in your life. These are people who will respect and value you and your accomplishments. You may not have much contact with your family and previous friends because you may find that they judge you - here again, courage is going to be required to live through this time as well. Wisdom and freedom are often hard won.

As you use your courage to stand up for yourself, you will find that this delicious and amazing new feeling, this courage thing, begins to live within you. Now, more and more, you are not afraid of really anything. You stand up for others when you can. You can feel yourself growing.

Eventually you die, you review your life and you get to see how much progress you made in this most recent life. You will get to see what else you want to learn and how else you want to progress.

Now you will not have to just do it over, you can live in a totally new way in the next incarnation with new people and new opportunities.

Now you are acquiring wisdom and advancing on your path of soul evolution, which is the point of living and learning in each new life you live.

## The Karmic Opportunity

The acquisition of wisdom is hard won.

You will have an experience until you learn the lesson that created the experience in the first place.

When you no longer need an experience, it ceases.

When you no longer need a particular type of person in your life, that personality type will no longer be with you.

See yourself pondering each new situation with a wiser eye toward changing the future.

## Affirmation

## The Lightworker's Guide to

Every day I pray for the wisdom to make the right choices on my karmic path.

## Week 7   We Become Our Parents

What is the point of a spiritual path, if it is not to understand who we are, where we have come from and where we are all going, nowadays, at tremendous speed?

What is the point of looking back at our childhoods and evaluating what we learned from those early days of mortal life if it is not to appreciate what we learned from our parents?

There is a theory that we pick our parents, and parents pick their children, purely for the lessons that we are going to learn from each other. If this is the case, then what is the reason we picked the parents we did in this mortal life we call now, if not to specifically seek to change those generational patterns?

The point, the reason is that if we do not learn from our parents, if we do not consciously seek to change the pattern of our parents [if it was a negative pattern], and often grandparents, then for the next one thousand years, people will still be abusing, yelling, avoiding issues, or failing to provide support for their children and staying in denial of what is happening all around them.

# The Lightworker's Guide to

A thousand years is a very long time. Perhaps this story may help to illustrate the point. This is the true story of the Navy Petty Officer who beat his wife. He was an excellent Petty Officer. He got all kinds of awards because he was hard working, conscientious and loyal to the Navy. However, he was not loyal to his family. This seemingly great guy just beat the devil out of his wife. So the Navy, in its infinite wisdom sent this man to anger management school. They sent him to a Navy psychiatrist. They also took him to Non-Judicial punishment for Conduct Unbecoming a Petty Officer because of the violence he perpetrated against his wife.

Despite all of this attention to his problem, he still beat his wife. Then one day, after all of this focus on retraining him had utterly failed, he sat down to talk to his Executive Officer, who happened to be female.

"Commander, I just do not understand, so I beat my wife, what's the big deal? Nobody's perfect."

Imagine how utterly incensed his Executive Officer must surely have been as she stared across her desk at this sailor who is calmly telling her that he really sees nothing wrong in beating his wife. To her credit, she did not scream at him. She just sat for a moment and then she asked him some questions.

"Petty Officer Jones, did your father beat you when you were a kid?"

"Yes Ma'am! He surely did, all the time, mostly every day he'd tan my hide but good!"

"Petty Officer Jones, did your grandfather beat your father?"

"Yes Ma'am! He surely did! My grandfather beat my father till he plumb couldn't stand up!"

Then he became really thoughtful and finally he said:

# Everyday Karma

"Commander, doesn't everyone get beaten when they grow up?"

What was this man really saying when he finally voiced this statement: "….doesn't everyone get beaten when they grow up?" Perhaps what he was asking was that isn't abuse part of everyone's pattern? Why his father was just doing what his grandfather did and his father before him and for possibly the previous one thousand years, family members had beaten each other and literally thought nothing of it. Blindly they had all just perpetuated this abusive family pattern.

Finally, as kindly as she could, his Commander explained that no, not every one gets beaten when they grow up. There are those families who do not beat each other. There are families who respect and love each other and do not perpetrate violence against one another. But violence was all he had ever known. He was completely bewildered. He thought he was supposed to become like his father. If he did not become like his father, how else would he behave? He had no idea that to stop beating his wife, he would have to stop becoming his father. He would have to change the future for the next thousand years.

How does this story end? No one knows, for soon after this conversation, Petty Officer Jones got transferred and his Commander never saw him again, never knew if that simple conversation changed the future for that family legacy for the next thousand years.

The point of a spiritual path is to carefully and consciously analyze, without judgment, the things our parents did. We must decide if those are the things we will want to emulate. If they are not, then we will have to make a conscious effort to watch ourselves to see if we are becoming our parents. Are we sarcastic, inconsiderate, cruel, abusive, needy, childlike, in denial of reality, cowardly - just like them? Are we loyal, considerate, thoughtful, conscientious, and generous on every level and, above all, wise - just like them?

We are a combination of the best and the worst of our parents. We picked these parents because of all the lessons they are teaching us. However, if we do not identify what the lesson is, we cannot possibly learn it. If we cannot identify the lesson, we cannot possibly change that pattern. We will become our parents unless we make an extremely conscious effort to change that reality. Perhaps we had great parents. No problem. Perhaps we had parents who did the very best they could and that included mimicking the behaviors of their parents.

Part of the opportunity for the 'New Age' is the opportunity to see the end of something, hopefully the old patterns of action and to welcome the coming of the new patterns of action. The most wonderful patterns we could possibly create are the ones deeply steeped in the wisdom of the past recast with the hope of the future. Combine this with a profound willingness to change and open up to a thousand years of peaceful mortal life.

## The Karmic Opportunity

Analyze why you picked your parents.

What lessons have they taught you?

What is your family's emotional pattern?

How have you changed your karmic path for the better?

Are you becoming your parents?

## Prayer

## Everyday Karma

Heavenly Father, I pray that I may have the wisdom to appreciate my family and all the lessons that they have taught me. Amen.

The Lightworker's Guide to

## Week 8    Spiritual Charades

Throughout history, there have been people who have claimed that they could talk to God and that God spoke back to them. Many people believed what these people said they heard, thinking that God must have said something like: "On the 15th of March do this or that at about 10:00 am and wear this and use this tool and use these people." Few messages from the Divine are ever that clear much less that specific. Some people decide to do something and God has nothing to do with it.

Some people believe that psychics are hearing God or 'Spirit' tell them things. This is especially true of fortunetellers. Often, people will give very good money for a "reader" to tell them their future because they believe that somehow the psychic has a better connection to the Divine than anyone else ever could. However, if we really listen to the answer any "seer" has, it is always vague because if they are the real thing, what they are going to hear if they even can hear anything, is just a vague answer, perhaps a direction and that is all. If it is exceptionally specific, then this is probably not God talking, but the psychic. No divine messenger will ever interfere with free will, so yes or no answers are pretty iffy.

# Everyday Karma

Those of us who consider ourselves ordinary people would like to be able to talk to God and listen to the gentle reply. However, the problem most of us have is learning how to listen and discerning what we are hearing. We wonder if we can even attempt to talk to God beyond the concept of prayer. We all understand that prayer is the language of God, but what about other avenues? Do they exist as well?

Every mortal soul can talk to God. We are all wearing the luscious red shoes of Oz fame. We just forget to look at those humble feet in those gorgeous shoes and realize that we have the power within us to communicate with the Divine. Like Dorothy, all we really need is a good teacher to show us the way, to unlock the mystery of those red slippers. We also need to believe that we can talk to God and find that bridge to Divine communication.

What are the steps to building this Divine communication bridge? They are really quite simple. We must each raise our frequency to higher and higher levels. We all vibrate at certain frequencies and the higher the frequency, the easier it is to hear all the Divine Assistants, who are on the other side. Raising frequency is about being happy, being in love with life itself and loving all the wonderful people in our lives. The more joy we can each feel, the more gratitude and love we can send out, the higher our frequency will be as a purely natural outcome. The higher our frequency is, the easier it will be to actually hear the higher realms.

Let us say that we have raised our frequencies, and now we are working on communicating with the Divine. How do we know how to discern what it is we are actually hearing? This is a really hard question.

Sometimes we are not quite sure what we think we heard. Sometimes it just feels like spiritual charades.

In the game of charades, we are trying to discern what someone else is trying to tell us, using hand signs and symbols. "Sounds like. . . ." as we point to our ear or "3 words. . ." as we hold up 3 fingers. Sometimes we dance all around trying to get the other person to 'get it.' The game is virtually always frustrating. We use lots of 'signs and symbols.' Lots of people give up, and lots of people give up trying to hear the faint, ephemeral voice of God.

Perhaps we have asked ourselves: "Why doesn't God just come out and tell me what I am supposed to do in this situation? Why is hearing all of this so hard!?" Even if a person is able to go deep into a meditation, the challenge is always the aspect of discerning what we are supposed to do, hear, say, or learn. Truly, why is this so hard?

The answer is that the cosmic-faint whisper of the voice of God, the words of the Divine, are just that, a whisper, a subtlety. God makes us work very hard to hear this voice because He does not dictate to us. He does not abrogate free will. He also offers us the answer in a thousand subtle ways through all kinds of signs, symbols and mechanisms. Our task is to be able to translate that language of God. There is not one Rosetta stone with all the translated answers. We have to work much harder than that to hear what is being said; however, it is possible to learn this language.

The first mechanism for communicating with the Divine is through the sleep state, and one of the simplest ways to communicate is to ask a question of our Higher Self, God or our Guardian Angel with a prayer of gratitude right before we fall asleep. It is wise to request guidance or wisdom, not a yes, or no answer. As we awaken, allow the precious moments to let whatever guidance we did receive to come into our awareness. As we write down what we think we "heard," we need to see how we feel about what we think we understood. Does it ring true? Do we feel peaceful when we think about it? Often, the best answers are a greater insight into a problem rather than a specific answer. Then using this insight, we can take wiser action.

It is always important to seek the acquisition of wisdom. Wisdom by itself is a connection to the Divine. Wisdom by its very nature helps us get ourselves out of the way and allows us to see all the facets of a situation without the confusing cloud of emotion. The less emotion we have regarding a situation, the more clearly we can hear the wisest approach to the problem. Violent, negative emotions automatically lower our frequencies. This is why, when seeking wisdom, setting emotion aside is a powerful action. It is not always easy and we may not always feel successful about it all the time, but at least we can try. Once these emotions are either worked through or released, we may be able to feel more balanced and able to connect to the Divine on a clearer level.

A second mechanism for connecting to the Divine is looking for signs and symbols. There are entire metaphysical books detailing spiritual signs and symbols, so the following are but a few examples:

- If you see hawks or eagles as you are driving, you may feel that you are being protected by a higher power. The more of these powerful symbols of protection you see, the more powerful you may feel that protection to be.
- Lots of vermin, flies, fleas, ticks, gnats, poisonous spiders and mice or rats signify a

greater level of negativity. Something dark is attracting them. Cleaning may remove that source. These creatures, are a sign that something needs to be cleaned on many levels.

- Several signs can mean a change is about to occur in your life, one is moving trucks everywhere you look, funeral processions, or hearses. Either of these can mean that something is about to end and something new is about to appear in your life. Hearses do not always mean death, although they can mean that someone close to you may be nearing death.

- Everywhere you go you meet the nicest people. People say nice things to you and things work out well for you most of the time. This may symbolize that your frequency is rising and people are recognizing your goodness; they are feeling comfortable and delighted in your presence. It can also mean that you are in resonance with higher frequency people and you may no longer need the experiences of so many problems.

- If you have lots of legal problems, dealing with lawyers can mean that you are surrounded by lots of negativity. The very thought of having to deal with the legal system makes most people tense, angry, often powerless and lowers frequency. This is quite a powerful symbol.

- Fire trucks, ambulances, police cars, with sirens blaring, flashing warning lights, can mean several things. One is to be very careful as you move forward because there is danger ahead, slow down and be mindful of the steps you take. Another possible meaning is that something you may have done has angered people on some level and it may be necessary to literally "put the fire out" or "cool things down."

- Problems with water can mean a variety of things. Water represents the subconscious and when you have water problems, your subconscious is trying to tell you that there is a problem. Toilets backed up [more than on rare occasions] mean that there is something dark inside you that you need to heal. Water overflowing or flooding can mean that you are feeling overwhelmed in your life. Spilling liquids [more than one time] can mean that you are out of balance and must stabilize things.
- Dead batteries, especially your car battery, mean that you are out of energy and are extremely tired. It can also mean that something or someone may be draining you of your energy.
- Warning lights are great because they cause you to slow down, pay attention to something that you are obviously missing and need to watch.

The examples above are classic examples of spiritual charades. Each symbol can mean several things. The challenge is discerning what they mean in a given situation and bringing that situation or emotion to the surface to deal with it in a balanced confident manner. If you see a challenging sign, show courage, not fear.

Hearing God is a process of bringing all the parts of each of us back into some sort of balance and keeping them there. The more effort we put into seeking to understand the symbols and process this meaning, the more balance we will have and the easier it will be to become elegantly more successful at this eternal game of spiritual charades.

## The Karmic Opportunity

Everyone has the same spiritual opportunity to speak to God.

What spiritual signs are you seeing?

Be willing to think outside the standard spiritual thought box and see life a bit differently.

Work on raising your frequency by focusing on the positive.

Remember to record your waking thoughts and dreams.

## Prayer

Heavenly Father, I pray that I may always be open to the knowledge, wisdom and light of the Divine. Amen.

# Week 9   Look for the Reason

Everything happens for a reason. This is an important metaphysical tenant based on karmic law: for every action there is an equal and opposite reaction. Hence, when something happens, perhaps it would be good to at least think about the reason that this has happened.

This concept is not designed to make you feel paranoid about every little thing, but there are events that offer you an opportunity to study why things happen. This includes everything from death to leaky pipes [explained below], winning the lottery to having a long and happy marriage. Some important things just are an effect of some specific cause.

Carry this concept a little further and you then embrace the concept that everything you do influences/affects something else. Sometimes you go about your day and are not consciously aware that you are intending for something to happen or that you are influencing something, but you are. When you study Feng Shui, you become aware of the concept of intention. In Feng Shui, you intention objects to perform specific functions for you, be they mirrors, crystals or Foo dogs, which are the usual Feng Shui items.

## The Lightworker's Guide to

For a beginner in Feng Shui, this often seems silly. However, the Chinese know that whatever you focus your intention on takes on the focus of your energies. So, if you intention the Foo dogs to protect you, you are focused on that, or have that intention every time you pass them. Eventually, you feel more protected. You may then sleep better, in turn making you feel better and better. The more rested you feel, the more confident you feel, which means that you may do your job better and get noticed, which could also lead to a promotion. Everything is connected. So if you look at the concept that you were promoted, the reason may be a combination of intentions you made some time ago.

Now let us look at leaky pipes. As you just learned in the above Feng Shui example, many times events and objects are symbols of something else and can mean something else. Let us say the pipe under your kitchen sink is leaking. In the case of leaky pipes, loss of water means loss of energy, whether it is a large drain and or a slow dripping drain. Find the problem, fix it and you may get insight into something that is draining your energy in your daily life. You may also find that your finances improve!

Sometimes looking for the reason for an event may cause you to avoid a place of judgment. When something happens, perhaps in the past you would rush to judgment and say that this or that happened because you were careless, dumb, or reckless. But what if you withheld that judgment and simply dealt with the situation in front of you without judgment? Then guilt would not be part of the equation. Without guilt, healing is significantly faster, pain is less and the person feels more open to share perhaps the real reason something happened. Not rushing to judgment will open the possibility of other explanations, which may emerge over time. Rash judgments will reduce anyone's willingness to talk about what happened to them.

Withholding judgment will preclude looking at any situation as tragic and unfair. Every situation is fair because karma sees it with a balanced eye, even situations where a small child is dying, or dies. Patience in looking for the reason will stand each of us in good stead for the long haul. In a situation where you do not get a promotion, maybe someone else needed that experience more than you needed that experience. What if your candidate doesn't win a particular election? Maybe history had other plans and you are not privy to those plans. Another element here is that many things happen and you cannot fathom why something happened when and how it did. What you cannot reasonably be expected to see is how whatever has occurred has satisfied a karmic need for balance. Even the death of a precious loved one may be balancing karma in the critical lesson it teaches.

If you do not look for the underlying cause of any situation, how can you prevent that situation from reoccurring? You probably cannot prevent its happening again. Which would mean that you did not embrace the lesson that the first occurrence offered. Once you learn the lesson, really take the lesson to heart, then while karma will test you to be sure you got the message, eventually that particular lesson does not need to be repeated.

You would be wise to give yourself a break and take the time to look for the reasons that things happen. Perhaps the real benefit will be greater insight and a less stressful life.

The Lightworker's Guide to

## The Karmic Opportunity

Be more mindful of the focus of your intention.

Practice withholding judgment and just observe the moment.

Relinquish guilt now and forever.

Remind yourself that karma is always fair even when you feel that your heart is breaking.

Everything that happens occurs for your greater good. Look for that learning experience to manifest at some point in the future.

## Affirmation

Everything that happens will eventually have been for my greater growth and insight.

## Week 10    Car Karma

### Owning a Car

As many of you know, my oldest son, James is a Master Mechanic for BMW. Both of my brothers, although in different careers, are also brilliant at understanding cars. Listening to these wonderful car-loving guys over the years has taught all of us a great deal about cars: why they work, why they do not and how we influence how our cars perform. Cars literally are karma in action. What you do or don't do to your car comes back to you sometimes in astonishing ways.

Most really good auto mechanics are at least a little psychic. Many do not know it, but they are. They have a feeling about a car, what is wrong with it or how it feels about its owner. Some cars will actually tell a mechanic that they hate their owner – which is why they are in the shop all the time needing attention!

When the mechanic speaks to the owner, they will frequently hear the owner say that they just hate this car, it is nothing but trouble, they should not have bought this car, it never runs right, what a heap!

Like a doctor questioning a worried parent about a child, the service writer/mechanic at a dealership will question you about this extremely complicated piece of machinery called your car and ask you what problems you are experiencing.

What the mechanic or service writer is actually hearing is that there is a disharmony between the car and its owner. People who hate their cars send the car an energy frequency of hate. If you stand next to someone who hates you, you can feel it. Well, your car can feel that you hate it every single time you get in it and turn it on. It can feel that you do not care about it or do not value it because you do not take care of its most basic needs. Those basic needs will be discussed a bit later.

How can you have a good relationship with your car? Follow these basic rules:

- Keep your car clean. We bathe because we get rid of not only surface dirt, but also psychic debris – this is also true for cars. A car will run/work better if it is clean inside and out. If your car is full of trash and clutter, this speaks volumes about what is going on in your life. You literally are overwhelmed with that which is bringing you difficulty.
- Never allow trash in your car. The trunk should be clean and spotless. If you have little kids, teach them to help keep the car clean. As a side note, open your mail in your house and not in your car. Some people have actually damaged their credit ratings because they forgot that their bills were in their car and forgot to pay them. Also, some identities have been stolen through the theft of personal bills and mail. If this means that you have to change a habit, give this some serious thought and bring your mail into your house.

- Love your car. Tell your car that you love it. Thank your car for getting you from one place to another.
- Bless your car by asking that your car be blessed and be kept safe from negative things. Change the energy between you if it has not been positive. Apologize for past negative thoughts.
- Care about this piece of sophisticated metal. We know that stones have energy. Well, autos are made up of all kinds of minerals, from iron and steel to aluminum and gold. There are even quartz crystals in the computer chips. All of these minerals carry an energy imprint given them by whoever is with them the most.
- Keep your car clean. Detail it as often as possible. Do not too be busy to care for your car. Always ensure that your car looks like a million dollars!
- Your vehicle represents your freedom in life. Honor your vehicle because it represents the method by which you move into the future. Look at this amazingly complicated piece of machinery as a critical part of your life and love this vehicle.

## Auto Maintenance

Being very honest, I must put myself at the head of the list of people who do not love having to take care of auto maintenance. In fact, while we were living in Italy, I suggested expansively to the mechanic who was putting gas in my speedy, red, Fiat that he check the oil. He looked at me astonished: my car had no oil. Yet, it ran. I just loved that very fast, red Fiat. Needless to say, oil was added and I took better care of my car after that.

## The Lightworker's Guide to

Actually, that car should not have run without oil, but it did. I think it took care of me and finally I heard its pleas for oil.

If you want your car to be good to you, here are some tips from my son, James, on what all of us should be taking care of in our cars – whether or not you own a BMW.

- Check the oil in your car at least once a month – if you do not know how, learn how. Keep a log of when last the oil was last changed and when you should change it again. Learn the oil weight to use and always, always replace the oil filter when you change the oil.
- Check all fluid levels, transmission, power steering as well as oil and windshield washer fluid. Some newer luxury cars have sealed transmissions and do not need this fluid changed. If your car is older than three years old, check on this.
- If you do not have a sealed battery, then check the water level in the battery and fill it with distilled water only.
- If you have a radiator, check the fluid level here. If you live in a state with a cold climate, then you will have to check the antifreeze/fluid level as well. Always use distilled water in your radiator.
- Clean the leaves that collect under your windshield wipers. A small detail, but the leaves that collect here eventually get stuck in the ventilation area of the car. With moisture, they rot and create terrible smells in your car. If you wash your car frequently, this problem will be eliminated.

# Everyday Karma

- Tire pressure is really critical. Find out what the correct pressure for your tires should be, it is written either in the door of the car [for some luxury cars] or on the tire itself. Correct tire pressure will dramatically improve gas mileage. On some luxury cars, front tires have a different tire pressure than back tires.
- Check for wear on your tires and rotate them periodically. This keeps them in good shape and extends the life of the tire. Some tire shops will do this for free if you buy your tires there.
- Use good gas in your car. Most mechanics use premium in their cars because they know what the engines look like with poor gas, especially gas from really cheap dealers.
- Obvious as this is, do respond to the 'check engine' or 'service engine soon' lights on your dashboard. They are there for a reason. This is one method your car uses to talk to you.
- Fluid leaks seen on your garage floor or driveway must be addressed. They are a symptom of a growing problem. You may have to have belts and hoses replaced if you have an older car.
- Older cars will have to have an air conditioning service done.
- If your car has a timing belt – such as a Nissan – get this replaced on a scheduled plan. If this belt breaks, you could be looking at a whole new engine. A belt is so much cheaper.

Sounds like a lot to do, but if you schedule hair and nail or golf and massage appointments, why not include your car in that list of important things to do? It could save you thousands of dollars over time.

Consider this true story. In 1972, a single lady bought a brand new Nissan 240Z. Because she knew nothing about cars, she did exactly what the dealership told her to do with her car. She took it in for every single scheduled maintenance checkup that the dealership suggested – on time. She spent the money on the car required to care for it. She developed quite a relationship with the dealership and her car over many years. Eventually, her car hit 600,000 documented miles on the original engine, which was so unusual, that this fact was reported to Nissan. Nissan asked to meet with this lady and asked her to 'swap' her old 'Z' for any brand new car Nissan made. She accepted. They had never had a customer take such good care of a car as she had and they wanted to study the engine. What they ended up studying was the concept of car care done faithfully. They probably did not consider the fact that she adored her car – which we who study metaphysics would appreciate. In the end, she and her car were (actually and karmically) rewarded handsomely for the care they took of each other. Car karma in action absolutely works!

## Buying a New Car

Most people decide to buy a car when the old one breaks down and they are in a panic to get something that runs so that they can get to work. If it has never happened to you, you are most fortunate. However, it may have happened to a lot of people at one time or another. This is one of the primary reasons people hate their cars. They were in a terrible hurry when they bought them, and they took what they could get at a price they could afford and they had no bargaining position at all. They then became somewhat angry about the vehicle they ended up with. They were also mad at themselves.

# Everyday Karma

They had known for a while that their car was in bad shape, but they hoped it would limp along for a bit longer because they could not afford anything new. They did not want to pour money into the car and do the maintenance and then all of a sudden they are faced with something major: either fix it or buy a new car. You know you are facing the purchase of a new car when the monthly cost of fixing the one you have is approaching the cost of a new car payment.

People who love their cars purchase their cars when they are in a power position. This sounds strange, but it makes a big difference. Being in a power position means that you do not necessarily need a new car. However, being a realist, you have analyzed your position and you can see what is ahead of you. You decide to pick your time to purchase because you have the wealth [of mind] and the luxury of time to really, really shop for the car you are ready to have. The car you think you want may not be the car you end up with. Whatever that car is, you have to love it because you are going to be making payments every month on it or you are going to have paid for it in full with a check. This is the second biggest dollar value purchase people make and they usually do it in a panic. This frequently leaves them quite unhappy with the outcome.

Most people buy at least seven cars in their lifetime. Decide that your experience will be great and that you will have the car you just love. Also, do not discount owning a brand new or pre-owned luxury car: BMW, Cadillac, Lexus, Jaguar, Mercedes or Infiniti, etc. There are some tremendous buys on these and owning a luxury car tells you that you are worthy of wealth. The car you drive represents you and how you think of yourself and will definitely influence how others see you.

Here are some simple tips for buying a new car:
- Shop until you drop. Shop for a year if you have to. Drive every single model car there is and keep a logbook. Do it for fun. Do it when you do not need to. Just do it. Go ahead and get confused. Drive the same car several times. Imagine that car in your garage. Imagine that you own this car.
- Decide what you want to choose to spend. Research insurance costs. Know what you are looking at pricewise. Get over sticker shock. If you have not purchased a car in 10-16 years, some of the prices will take your breath away. Get comfortable with what cars cost today.
- Look at leasing. Talk to your accountant. Decide what is best for you.
- If you are looking at pre-owned, go to www.kellybluebook.com and find out what the blue book value of that car is, based on the amenities it has. This will help your bargaining position when you decide to begin negotiating.
- Read Consumer reports about the types of problems your dream car could potentially have. Decide if that is OK with you.
- Remember there are all types of cars out there because there are all types of people and we live in a country with astounding choices before us. Sometimes those choices are bewildering, but blessedly, we have them.
- If you are terrible at negotiating, take someone who has no agenda but getting you a good deal and then let them do their job.
- Car negotiating is an art. You only do it a couple of times in your life. Car salesmen do it every day.

## Everyday Karma

It is arrogant to think you are really any match for these guys who are trained to get the best price for the dealership. However, someone who has no agenda is emotionally neutral to the car and can usually do a better job of negotiation.

- If you want to pay full price then your job will be easy. If you enjoy negotiating, keep in mind that the car you are negotiating for is not the only car in the world. Be prepared to walk away from it if you have to. Decide what you really want to spend.
- Once you own the car, pay close attention to the service intervals for your car. Mark your calendar if necessary to check on things in your car.
- Learn what the gadgets in your car do. This sounds really obvious but do not decide to learn how the windshield wipers work when it starts to rain.
- Give your car a name that is beautiful. Refer to your car by that name. It will make a difference.
- Feng Shui your car. There are many books on this. Use Feng Shui mirrors to deflect negativity from your car.
- Clean out your garage in preparation for this new energy in your life. Make sure there is plenty of space to house it and to care for it.
- Now, watch what happens when you drive it. Watch how your life just feels better.
- Finally enjoy this lovely new car: you earned it! Know that you are worthy of this wonderful machine and just have a blast!

## Miscellaneous Car Info

## The Lightworker's Guide to

Sometimes there are just things you should know about cars that will help you to do a better job of being a car owner.

Washing your new car requires special attention. My sons have adamantly informed me that you never, ever use dish or clothes washing soap on a new car. These soaps have a certain level of abrasive and bleach in them, which is terrible for the clear coat finish on the paint job of automobiles. There is a special soap that is used that protects the clear coat and is sold at dealerships or automotive shops.

Car Wash places are fine for older cars, especially if that is all that you can do to keep your car washed is spend $10 going through the car wash. Once you have a new car, then you will need to hand wash it with the special soap mentioned above. If you do use a car wash machine make sure that it is touch free.

Eating in cars is really an American phenomenon. Japanese and Europeans, especially German drivers, do not eat in their cars. This is why their cup holders are woefully inadequate [especially in any Volkswagen or BMW]. Foreign car manufacturers consider eating and driving dangerous, (imagine that!) and not recommended when driving. This is worth considering. The number of auto accidents in Europe is far less than the United States because Europeans just drive. They do not talk on cell phones, eat, play the flute or comb their hair while driving. They just drive. They drive really fast and they know they need to concentrate.

Keep the inside of your car clean by simply taking your stuff with you when you get out of your car.

Keep your trunk empty and clean with a few helpful things left in it like a blanket for protecting your trunk or keeping you warm if you need it.

Finally, love your car. Listen to your car. Someday, we will all have "a relationship" energetically with our machines; they will be sentient creatures because we will understand that the energy that created them is still there and can be positively or negatively influenced. You can start that relationship today by saying -- while in your car -- that you love your car. Love heals and causes all energetic things to thrive whether they are kids or cars, pets or plants. Your car will karmically repay your love a thousand-fold and you will feel safer and happier when you drive it.

## The Karmic Opportunity

Love and honor your car and keep it clean inside and out.

Bless your car by asking that your car be blessed and be kept safe from negative things.

Keep up the maintenance on your car, oil, fluids, belts and hoses, etc.

Love your tires they are the feet of your car, check pressure, wear and rotation.

Take your time before buying a car. Never buy one in a hurry.

Feng Shui your new car and/or your old one, to always keep it protected and in balance.

Use a touch free car wash or do it yourself, with special car soap.

## Prayer

Dear Lord, please bless this car and all who ride in it. Protect it from anything negative and thank you for the blessing that this car is to me. Amen.

The Lightworker's Guide to

## Week 11   Training Wheels

When we were little kids, one of the rites of passage in growing up was learning to ride a bike. Some of us took longer to learn this than others. Some of us were never given training wheels to steady us, but we had someone run alongside for a while, acting like training wheels. Hopefully, we all sooner or later learned to ride: the path to getting there was unique to each of us.

We built our confidence with the loping parent and/or the training wheels. Eventually we were OK when the training wheels came off. Sooner or later our confidence was strong enough for us to ride all on our own. We even strengthened our courage to ride up the big neighborhood hill and even take the risk of crashing when we came down it as well.

But there are some people who did not have a parent who, for whatever reason, could run along side of them. Some of them had to learn on their own. Some of them never learned. Riding a bike is just one of those seemingly insignificant childhood rites of passage that dramatically builds confidence. It is a success brick that you use to build your foundation for your house of confidence and emotional security.

# Everyday Karma

Some people never had anyone teach them how to make those success bricks. So many of them tried, so many of them looked deep within themselves and tried to overcome the inadequacy of their parents. Some tried but just lacked the internal mechanism to understand how to be successful.

We have all met these people, people who just were given little or nothing in childhood and they cross our path and we ponder how do we help them? What can one person do?

Perhaps the answer is to be that person's training wheels, even for just a little while. This means that we believe in that person.

Schoolteachers do this all the time, which is why some schoolteachers are so memorably precious to us.

What does it mean to believe in someone? It means that we say it out loud: I believe in you. I believe that you can do it. I trust you. I see something in you that tells me you are a good person. I believe you have what it takes to do this project.

Perhaps this person did not start out with a good foundation, but it does not mean that there is no hope for them. It means that when a person whom we are seeking to assist asks for guidance, we listen beyond the basic question. We listen to their need for approval, their need to earn successes, even little ones at first. Self-esteem has to be earned to be a foundation success brick.

Unconditional praise that is honestly given and honestly earned is precious. It is more valuable than gold and yet it is golden because it is a facet of love. There are only two emotions: love and fear and all other emotions evolve from these two. Hence, teaching a person success techniques means loving them and loving the process of their success. It means that we have to be secure enough within ourselves to give to another. It means that the other person is giving us a chance to share our success and to teach them what it feels like when someone else has trust and confidence in them.

Perhaps many of us remember the first time our parents allowed us to drive the family car. They believed in us. Their belief/confidence in us were those training wheels. Eventually, we could drive on our own. Or the first time we cooked an entire meal for the family and everyone loved it - no fault was found. The memory of that flush of quiet pride is so important.

Praise for a job well done is complete. It is not faint praise: "This would have been good if only you had done this or that." This is a success/confidence destroyer. Criticism is never constructive. Learn how to build confidence by finding things that you can say that are really well done. Set the person up for success. Then follow through with praise. The next time, they will achieve the success on their own and the follow on praise will be well earned.

What can one person do to help another person? Be the training wheels for their success. This is a major deposit in our karmic savings and loan account. We just cannot imagine what wonderful things we will receive as a return on that karmic investment!

## The Karmic Opportunity

Service is often acting like the training wheels for another person.

Give complete praise. Always avoid faint praise.

Look for the goodness in another person and then focus on that goodness to build confidence.

Have the patience to listen to what the person in front of you really needs.

## Affirmation

I have the patience to be the training wheels for those who need me.

I have the wisdom to know when to help and to know when to let go.

The Lightworker's Guide to

## Week 12    Gratitude

Did you ever notice that people seem to take things that are done for them for granted? We all live in a time when old-fashioned courtesy just seems out of vogue. Even one of the automatic answering machines with some companies felt that they could save money and time by removing the kindly greeting and the "thank you for calling" at the end.

We have all experienced doing things for others and we know that they are not going to acknowledge it. Sometimes we decide that it goes with the territory. We earned the karma for it and that will have to be enough. It irritates us that what we did was not acknowledged, but we live in the real world and we probably do not acknowledge what others do for us as much as we should either.

This is why thank you notes, those irritating little duties, are really important because that little note acknowledges that someone took the time and effort to pick something out for us, that they thought of us and it fuels our desire to do it again in the future. That little piece of paper makes us feel appreciated.

What if you do something really large for someone, not because you expected some huge reward

# Everyday Karma

or financial payment but because you wanted to do it, because you felt it was important. Is something owed to you from the other party? Yes. The other party needs to acknowledge exactly what was done and how much it meant to them. However, the odds of this happening are usually pretty small, which creates a problem: the giving person feels as if their offering was not fully acknowledged - that what they gave was just taken for granted - as if they owed it to the receiver. Often the giving person made it look easy, they never complained and they just got it done efficiently and, sometimes, elegantly.

    This brings up a controversial question. Should you give if you feel inherently that what you are doing will not be fully appreciated? Sometimes you have no choice. You do it not because you expect a reward, but because it is the right thing. Again, you earn the karma for it, even if, at the time, you feel an imbalance. Karma always seeks balance and the energy spent has to be returned in some time and in some way. This brings us to a crucial question: what is the real essence of gratitude, of appreciation? The essence of gratitude is the acknowledgement that something was done for someone and that it was appreciated. Perhaps the best example of how this is handled well is through all branches of the United States military.

    The military teaches that exceptionally hard work or courageous action has to be acknowledged with some written form of appreciation. That is why the homes of military people are lined with these awards. The financial value of them is usually merely pennies, the frames are worth more than the pieces of paper or the ribbons the person wears, but the sentiment that these objects represent is priceless. This is why military people are so intensely loyal - they feel appreciated.

Many people complain that their companies do not acknowledge their dedicated service and, when to cut costs, they cut people and expect everyone else to "pick up the slack" as if the person they cut was, well, a slacker and their job did not really matter. If you have to do two jobs, you know for sure that that person's job really mattered. The company does not give a bonus, an awards ceremony, a special day off, nothing. Resentment of this type of greedy, corporate behavior is universal. We hear people discuss it daily. This may be why some people have no loyalty to their employer.

The answer to this may just be that we have to decide within ourselves that what we did was important and not look for outside validation. If you hate your job or a task requested to do, then either seek to adjust to it, not do it at all or decide to change your job. This may bring you to a much happier place in the long run.

So what can you do if you feel a gratitude imbalance? Say something. If that is not an option, then decide what you have learned from the situation and what you can or cannot do. Then be satisfied that you have done your best. Also decide how you will handle a similar situation in the future. No one can take advantage of you without your inherent permission. Decide what permission to give and what to decline. This is taking your personal power back and that can make life very much more balanced on the physical and emotional level.

## The Karmic Opportunity

Become the example by remembering to be grateful to people around you.

Find ways to let others know you appreciate them.

## Prayer

Dear Lord, I send my gratitude to you for the blessings I receive daily, for the wonderful people in my life and the powerful learning opportunities you have provided to me. Amen.

## Week 13    The Darkness Within

Do you ever ponder why things happen to people? Do you ever wonder why some people are involved in endless lawsuits, have chronic tragedy/dramas, health problems or illnesses that occur one after the other? Some people look at life in a way that says that the world is against them, poor me or I'm just tired of living.

Some people look for the significance in each event and try to learn from each event. What separates people who spiritually advance and people who stay where they are is the ability to look at themselves as part of the fabric of the problem and do not blame other people. This does not mean the spiritual path seeker is a martyr. It means that he or she does not take everything personally, but works diligently at getting him or herself out of the way. They look for a different solution to problems that arise in the future.

In other words, they learn from each situation/lesson presented, looking for answers and then embracing the experience. They clear their own darkness because they are willing to change.

What is 'darkness?' It is fear, anger, or rage that we hang on to life after life. We are seldom aware we carry it, but we do. We do have the option of stepping back from life events and beginning to release those demons, by owning them and setting them free, replacing that dark part of ourselves with light. We have the option. The challenge is: will we change?

There are all kinds of movies out there that show a person who has been on a dark path have an experience that ultimately changes him or her. This event helps them to appreciate the detrimental life they have been living and make a conscious decision to change their life path. They begin to see the positive person they can become. It makes you wonder how many lives any of us have been living in darkness. What made this life different? Why has this person decided to change, now? Isn't it ironic that we all seem to roll over our darkness life after life, never really giving them up?

The actions that change our karmic path begin when we stop blaming and stop hurting others. Sometimes we have to slow down our actions before we can bring about change. Patience, courage and hope are the wellspring of change. Courage is always the first freedom because without courage, we do not believe in ourselves enough to believe we can leave the darkness. Patience allows us to work through a situation and hope enables us to believe we can have a different life.

How do you figure out what the darkness is that is inside of you? What if that darkness originated in a past life? You have several options. The first would be to begin to work with a good spiritual practitioner or enlightened psychotherapist. Stay with the person long enough to begin to unravel the traumas of childhood, the shocks and disappointments of life and the illnesses and injuries you may have experienced. Each event is connected. Each event will require healing. You may or may not need to look at a past life to understand what is happening in this life. The overriding element in this process is a willingness to take a different view of all that has happened to you. Your 'history' can be rewritten from the point of view of understanding the lessons karma was seeking to offer you. Once you do that, you begin to dispel darkness.

You can also try an experiment for a week: cease taking things personally, and step aside from events. Look at them in a detached way. See what discoveries can be made. Even such humble action can begin to positively change your karmic path.

## The Karmic Opportunity

Look at every life event as an opportunity to learn the lesson it inherently offers.

Refrain from taking things so personally.

Learn to recognize past patterns and vow to change how you react to any given situation.

Seek the wisdom necessary to resolve any problem.

## Affirmation

I have the courage it takes to change my life.

I always seek the wisest course of action, which will bring my life into balance and harmony.

## Week 14     The Many Faces of Ego

There are many forms of ego. You have seen pure arrogance - it is not necessary to describe it – which is perhaps the most obnoxious form of ego. For those on a spiritual path, this is not a form anyone would wish to pursue.

You have watched competitions where people vie to be the best, working feverishly to defeat another person or team. The problem with competition is that, to win, you have to hope desperately that someone else will fail. Karmically, this is a really negative practice. However, this aspect of ego, hoping that someone else will fail, is relatively easy to change. We simply ask that the person who needs the experience of winning the most, actually win. You can do your best and allow that the experience of winning may not always be in your best interests. By being genuinely happy for whoever does win, competing can be done in a balanced way. Sometimes you learn more by what does not work than by what does work. The energy of every experience, no matter how difficult, has precious value.

The student of metaphysics would always be wise to consider all aspects of ego in what he or she does. This can help you advance because you can see that ego is what frequently holds you back from being and giving another person your very best.

>What is Ego?
>Ego is impatience.
>Ego is arrogance.
>Ego is self-importance.
>Ego is frustration.
>Ego is self-degradation.
>Ego is knowing-it-all.
>Ego is criticism of self and others.
>Ego is expectation.
>Ego is not trusting, anything or anyone, except yourself.
>Ego is seeking to be perfect all the time.
>Ego is control.
>Ego is guilt.
>Ego is an essential element of fear.

And finally, Ego, among many other things, is judging yourself, another person, situation or outcome. If you engage in any of these attitudes then perhaps you may need to rethink how you go about doing the business of light work. If you are serious about your task, that of helping others, then your personal growth can be greatly enhanced by methodically working through each element of ego. If you can identify any of these aspects in yourself, then you have taken the first step in healing that aspect.

All Spiritual Workers must face and heal each of these aspects to advance in their tasks. It does not matter how long it takes to work through them, lifetimes if necessary, but work through them you must. If as you choose to work through them, you ask for help in achieving wisdom, insight and the cosmic view, a gentle miracle happens: help will be offered in some form. Ego may keep you from recognizing the humble way the answers, the solutions, the changes may be offered. Humility and a genuine desire to grow will enable you to find your way on your spiritual path.

And finally, when a student is ready, a teacher will appear. When you feel you have reached that point where you could benefit from more advanced work because you have in fact, gotten your ego out of the way, enjoy the presence and opportunity that teacher will provide. One of the things a good teacher will help to foster is the creation of confidence in your innate goodness. People often think that to release ego, they have to sacrifice confidence. This is untrue. Be confidently wise and enjoy the journey!

## The Karmic Opportunity

Seek to release ego as you proceed on your spiritual path.

Do not sacrifice confidence as you release ego, simply release the controlling fear-based elements of ego.

When a student is ready, a teacher appears.

Compete with patience and wisdom so that everyone has a chance at some point to feel that they can 'win' something.

## Prayer

Dear Heavenly Father, I pray for the wisdom to release ego and the confidence to move forward with my life in grace and happiness. Amen.

## Week 15    The Ego of Self-Importance

What is the difference between arrogance and self-importance? Perhaps the difference is slight. Arrogance is never seeing anyone else's needs, only your own. Self-importance is not necessarily arrogance; a self-important individual can see the needs of others, respond to them and be aware of them. Self-important people just assume that they are so important that their needs should come first. They also assume that you know how important they are.

This is frequently seen when you look at people in the public eye. Puffed up people who are filled with their own high opinion of themselves, believe that their requirement to have their needs answered first is acceptable behavior. They seldom want to know what it is going to cost someone else to fulfill that selfish person's need.

As you have heard a thousand times, you are here for service. Service is putting others first, not to your own detriment, but for the service of others. This is often a fine line because service workers can become quite tired from constantly giving. Someone doing or giving service must do a careful evaluation of what the situation is and how much they want to do, can do or will be allowed to do.

Often, a service worker can themselves become puffed up with their own self-importance. You sometimes see these folks in the clergy or the New Age movement on the talk show circuit. Their talk is always about themselves. But for those who are diligently working past the "me" stage, it is about the bigger picture. This is how you tell the difference. This is the shift in karmic focus of a true service/lightworker.

Take television personality Mr. Rogers, who did all of the shows about educating children. He was an ordained minister, but few people were aware of this until his death. His work for the betterment of children was all that mattered. In interviews, the focus was never about him, it was about the needs of children.

In a recent interview with Roma Downey, star of "Touched by an Angel," she was being asked about their last episode. Throughout the interview the focus was on the service of the series, the people who were touched and the service that had been performed. She was completely humble. Even the interviewer was almost confused because although she answered questions about herself, that was not her focus. The host was used to catering to self-important screens stars, not someone who put the mission first: Ms. Downey saw herself as the messenger, not the focus.

So, how about you? You are important. The needs of others are also important. Here again, getting yourself out of the way to see this very huge picture will help you keep your needs and the needs of those around you in perspective. Questioning what is happening and being sensitive is critically important. Focusing on the progress and the happiness of others is a delicate balance:

enjoy life; enjoy the progress and the happiness of others. Being genuinely happy for the success of another person is a true measure of getting ego out of the way. It is the service you would want for yourself. It is an excellent measure of how well you are evolving on your spiritual path.

## The Karmic Opportunity
Walk the path of a Lightworker with balance and controlled ego.

Remember the mission: service to others and personal spiritual growth.

## Affirmation
I walk the path of the Lightworker with confidence and a clear vision of the service mission.

## Week 16   Questioning God

There are some faiths that say it is a sin to question God. Why would that be a sin? When our children question us, as parents, do we not kindly and lovingly answer their questions? Do their questions not make us think and ponder our own lives? Are we not proud of our children for asking probing, intelligent questions?

So when one of us questions God, questions the infinite aspects of the Father, are we not seeking to understand that which is almost unfathomable? Doesn't this questioning put us in resonance with the Divine? For to understand the Divine, we have to feel it, know it, and want to have those aspects live within us.

What if the whole point of religion, of faith, is to question the workings of all that is? People want to know if there are ghosts, they want to know what happens after they die. So they ask about it. That is why there are so many books about the spiritual side of life. All these writers have questioning, probing, minds.

Does God punish people for questioning the workings of life and death, the reasons why one person lives and another dies? No. It is wonderful to think that we can ask anything we want, that we can probe with wonder all that we see and feel.

When there is a death of someone we love, we are often demanding of God to know why our loved one died. Eventually, in the end, we begin to get the answers – once we get beyond those hot, painful tears of grief. The answers come in dreams, in the sense of having angels around us. The journey of grief is one of teaching us to live more fully, because we have to learn to let go and to accept what we cannot change. Part of that process is questioning God.

The quest to know God is what drives us to know ourselves. We are one aspect of God. We are the creative output of the Divine Father made manifest in an infinite number of ways. To question God is to try to understand the balance of nature. Everything is balance. Imbalance is an aspect of contrast – perhaps it is why there is evil. How else can we know the difference? If there is no struggle, how do we know who we are? How do we figure out what defines us?

When will we get to know the answers to the endless questions that define life? When do we get to have a peek at the answers in the back of the book of life?

Perhaps if we have a broad concept of the afterlife, we can understand that when we leave the body, we have an opportunity to move into the heaven world. There we will find Counselors of Divine Wisdom who can help us with these answers. There are great and wonderful Masters who can help us to understand the more baffling aspects of our physical life. Perhaps we wanted to understand a physical ailment, a particular tragedy, or a world event. Perhaps we will want to understand why, no matter how hard we tried, we could not please a particular parent, our spouse or boss.

We can ask about life on other worlds, alien intelligence and just general questions about Universe administration.

Perhaps if we are a student of healing, we will want to understand the physical body differently. If we studied metaphysical philosophy we will be able to ask about the mosaic of how all the different belief structures fit together or how reincarnation works. And why do we have to come back again and again?

There are those of us who will want to understand the purpose and the lessons of evil. If we do not study this, how else can we make sense of all the atrocities in the world throughout history? Do we have to have war? Do we have to have sickness? Is this how Karma works?

So ask the questions now. Many answers will come forth, hopefully long before we move into the heaven world. Many answers await us. The more we ask, the more sophisticated the responses will be down the road.

We may also find out that there is a time when we do not come back to mortal bodies. That process will also be explained. What an amazing time that will be, for the Karma of repeated reincarnations of physical life on Earth will have been successfully completed!

## The Karmic Opportunity

Question God all you want.

Be patient for the ephemeral reply.

Seek wisdom from your questions, not just demand satisfaction.

Share the knowledge where appropriate with others as an aspect of exploring philosophy, not dogma.
Love the process of learning.

## Prayer

Heavenly Father, I pray for the light of Divine Wisdom so that I may understand the ways of the Universe and the balance of Karmic Law. Amen.

## Week 17    An Eye for an Eye

The law of Karma frequently confuses us because we hear people of ancient and current religions talk about the concept of 'an eye for an eye, a tooth for a tooth.' What does this mean? Does this mean that we sit in judgment of another who apparently has done a painful thing to someone and who is now going to pay for it in like manner by the judgment and actions of another person?

What if the 'eye for an eye, a tooth for a tooth' concept were misinterpreted? What if the real concept is Karma and Divine law simply balancing the scales of justice? What if this is not the job of mortal souls but the job of Divine justice? Would this then be in the purest sense absolute faith and trust in the Divine process?

After any horrific event, especially a terrorist attack or assault/murder of any kind, many people call for revenge and pray that the terrorists or murders will go to hell. Praying for a terrible thing to happen to another is black prayer and is simply wrong, no matter what someone else has done. Black prayer literally creates an intention and can put us in resonance with the very people with whom we are angry. Perhaps the best actions will continue to be to pray with all our hearts for the healing of the entire world, so that all souls will know love. We can also pray that healing will come to this planet as a Divine light. Any other action implies a judgment of events, which because of their bewildering complexity are in truth, beyond our total knowledge.

The fact is that we do not know what is karmically happening in various events. We do not know how Karma was working in that moment or how it will continue to work for the benefit of all the inhabitants of this planet. As we watch the news, we are aware of events that happen, but beyond that, we dare not judge, for that is not our job. Frankly, not judging is quite freeing, for we no longer have to decide, we just observe and do what we can do and move on. We can say a wonderful prayer for those who suffer and then get on with our lives. Dwelling on sadness is the creation of fear and depression. We can pray and then move forward with our day. We will have done all that can be done in that moment.

This is a critical element of trusting that the civil authorities will do a proper investigation and bring the perpetrators to some sort of justice through the only legal system we have. Using the legal system elevates all players so that we do not become like the terrorists or the murderers. The system of justice that balances the civil scales and removes individuals from continuing to cause harm is a far more dispassionate way to behave. It is the civilized way. Without the civilized way of life, we would return to a barbaric social construct, and anarchy would be the result. This legal process allows for the laws of Karma to operate on a day-to-day level. The eye for an eye, a tooth for a tooth type of justice eventually leaves everyone blind and toothless. The Divine Law of Karma brings about justice in a natural way, a way we may not anticipate or always understand. The scales of life are always balanced. We as mortals just have to have faith that this is so and become in resonance with the Divine laws of Karmic balance.

## The Karmic Opportunity

Reserve judgment of all horrific events.

Observe how the balance of karma works as a process.

Remember that your concept of justice may not be the essence of karmic justice.

Trust the process of karmic balance as an element of faith.

No matter how difficult a situation is, remember to open yourself to love, for only love heals.

## Prayer

Dear Father, open my eyes to the light of perfection of Karmic Law. Allow me to begin to understand this law so that I may follow it with a loving and wise heart. Amen.

The Lightworker's Guide to

## Week 18  Compassion Fatigue

You may seem to feel inundated with the speed at which things can happen to people. Sometimes it is a little thing, a disappointment, a problem, an accident, a health crisis, or a really big thing like a death or a natural disaster. If you are doing light work, it feels like you are riding your white horse hard and putting your steed away wet: you are using this steed so much! In other words, there is so much need to help, that you often feel like you are drowning in the sheer dimension, the numbers of problems people are experiencing. What you may be experiencing is a sense of compassion fatigue. Compassion fatigue is that feeling that you simply cannot hear one more sadness, one more horror or listen to one more person tell you about his or her grief. And yet, you are still called upon to help.

What can you do? Just listen. Most of the time you cannot solve the problem or change the fact that a disaster has happened, cannot make it better, cannot ensure that someone gets a promotion, or their child gets into that college they so desperately wanted, or gets the house they wanted. Sometimes all you can do is to listen so that the person blows off steam, so that he or she can be better because they did not hold on to the most toxic levels of their anger or despair. Sometimes it is all you

# Everyday Karma

can do to just listen with detached compassion. This alone is great service. It may not seem like it, but it is truly a service.

Believe it or not, the person talking to you really can get to the other side of their situation. You have to be patient with them while they make that journey. It is not your job to make everything perfect, to please everyone or to make each situation work out perfectly. Truthfully, you cannot possibly do that, great Masters cannot do that and even astoundingly capable multitasking mothers cannot do that. Sometimes situations happen because they are supposed to be that way so that something else will happen, so that you and they will learn. Learning comes at a price and, like making a monthly payment on a luxury car, you have to pay the price to enjoy the astounding experience that is the ride of life.

One of the hardest elements of assisting someone in a crisis is dealing with that person's tears. When someone is sobbing, it is a profoundly helpless feeling. All you want to do is get that crying to stop, get that person to dry their tears. You want to make it all better, kiss their finger and hope that it will all be OK. But sometimes it is important to accept that tears are part of healing, part of releasing the emotion of the moment.

Sometimes you just have to spend the emotional energy to learn the lesson, to accept what cannot be changed and to decide to move forward. Tears unspent back up in the body and make people emotionally constipated, literally they become full of awful stuff that is not being expended in a healthy way.

Tell the person if they are crying to go ahead and cry: give them permission to spend that energy in an emotionally healing way. Never tell someone to stop crying unless they are going nuts in front of a child. If that is the case, move them to another room. Some people respond to tears as if somehow they are like acid and create a feeling of inadequacy inside them. The truth is that the situation is seldom about you and totally about the other person. Get yourself out of the way and just listen, comfort and be compassionate. That may be the best you can do and, for the other person, that may be exactly what they need. That simple act of detached compassion is what light work is all about.

## The Karmic Opportunity

Do not be intimidated by tears. Tears are a healthy expression of emotional sadness.

Don't expect to have all the perfect answers to another person's problems.

Ask God to help you to know what to say in any given situation.

Request that an Angel of Peace and Calming be with that sad person.

Request an Angel of Wisdom for yourself.

Trust that all is happening in the right way and in the right time.

Recognize compassion fatigue and allow yourself to rest.

## Prayer

Heavenly Father, please grant me the strength and the wisdom to know what I can and cannot say in any given situation. Allow me to be an instrument of your Divine Light. Amen.

## Week 19  Maintaining the DNA Spiral: Intellectual/Emotional Factors, Specifically Friendships

What part do friendships play in your life when it comes to aging? It goes directly back to opening your heart to other people, letting them in and, frankly, being a friend. Again, in studies of people well over 100 they cited the ability to adjust to the changes that have come their way. The fact was that they depended on their friends to help them through it, not as a crutch, but so that they would allow others to share not only their grief and their sorrow, but also their joy and success.

If you feel alone in life, one of the prime factors that accompany this feeling is often fear. Fear flat-out ages you. It eats away at you and makes you look over your shoulder, feeling that there is no one you can trust. If you found that your parents were not trustworthy people, if they could not satisfy your needs as a very little child, they set you up for having a hard time making or being a friend. Babies are needy by definition and when that early neediness is satisfied, the person feels that the world is safe and can be trusted. When that infant neediness is not satisfied and that baby realizes that the adults entrusted by God to care for him or her cannot be trusted, then the child grows up feeling that he or she does not live in a safe world. Parents who do not keep their word and who are not consistently responsible create fearful, needy adults. These adults often have a hard time making and keeping friends.

If you were not encouraged to make friendships or never learned how to be a friend, you may find that you do not have friends.

You earn your friends. You earn the people in your life by that with which you resonate: the old 'birds of a feather. . .' situation. Well, with whom do you resonate? Do you resonate with people of good character, people who will be there for you if you need them? Are you that type of person for your friends?

Ask yourself if you would like a friend like yourself. So, the bottom line is, do you like yourself? Hopefully you do. Hopefully you look in the mirror and see a kind, caring person, a person who keeps their word, a person who can be trusted and a person who admits it if they make a mistake. Are you also a person who is capable of asking for help in an emergency? Are you a person who can be called on in an emergency, to change your priorities if the need arises? Will you put yourself last, to help a friend in a tough situation? If the answer to these questions is yes, then you probably have friends who will do that for you. You may also find that you have family members who will also step up to the plate on your behalf.

You create karma with everything you do. You especially create karma when you step into the role of a friend because, just like the roles of being a child, sibling, spouse or employee, friendship can be extremely challenging. Friendship requires that you think before you speak or act. It requires that you return the favors that your friends do for you and that you pay attention to the ever-present politics in any friendship situation. You edit what you say on occasion because that is what a good friend would do.

Now back to aging. Friends of all ages remind you that time does pass and that is a good thing. You may find that you do not have the same friends you had in college. Perhaps you changed and your collective lives changed. You may keep up, but new people do come into your life as you evolve. The best friends, the ones you keep the longest, are the ones who are also evolving, and these folks can include spouses and family members. The friends who choose to evolve also willingly face the future and do not retreat to constantly relive the past.

People who love the friends and family members in their lives also love life itself. They do not age quite as rapidly perhaps because they are not in a big hurry for their own life to be over. There is a unique pleasure in the sweet companionship of a cherished friend.

Aging is just another way to describe evolution, hopefully soul evolution. Everyone ages, but not everyone evolves. It is truly the lucky person indeed who does have friends who are evolving with them and who find joy in always making new friends while still honoring the old ones. Perhaps, when you are feeling thankful for your life, you might also give thanks not only for those wonderful friends who are still in your life after all this time, but also honor the new ones you have made over the last year. It is the thought of all these smiling faces and the warmth of their companionship that keeps your spirit young and your heart full of joy.

# The Karmic Opportunity

Use the lessons learned in childhood to become the friend you have always wanted to have.

Do not judge your friends. Learn detached compassion, so that you can be wise without being drowned by the drama of situations.

Build friendships over time by being a friend to people of all age groups because you are open to new ideas and thoughts.

Love all the people in your life for the pleasure they bring to you.

## Affirmations

I am the friend I want to have.

Whatever happened to me earlier in my life is making me a stronger and more compassionate person and an outstanding friend.

I love and cherish the people in my life and they love and cherish me.

Friends keep me young and involved in all the processes of soul evolution.

## Week 20   The Spiritual Philosophy of What Constitutes a Perfect Mother

No matter where you come from, somehow you are born with a spiritual philosophy of what constitutes a perfect mother. When your mortal mother does not live up to that spiritual philosophy, you begin to stack up her failings. Sometimes you identify a difficult father, but about 99% of the time, you instantly recount the failings of your mother. Why is this?

When you are in the heaven world, you look down on the parents you pick. If you can, you try to communicate with your mother. You also have a unique vantage point in the heaven world of seeing all the kinds of mothers out there and getting a good handle on what a fantastic mother should be. When you are born, you are sure you know what a perfect mother should be, and you are exceptionally sure of how to identify a bad mother. However, the reality is that we pick the mother we pick for the lessons she is going to teach us, no matter what kind of a mother she turns out to be.

The spiritual philosophy of what constitutes a perfect mother transcends all religions, all cultures and all times. A perfect mother, it turns out, is a perfect mother in all types of adversity. While there are nuances, these are the most universally accepted traits of a perfect mother.

## The Traits of a Perfect Mother

A perfect mother is the provider of unconditional love. She may not love what you do, but she will always love you, no matter what!

A perfect mother is courageous. She will stand up for you, will defend you from injustice and she will sacrifice herself for you because her love is so tremendous.

A perfect mother is a leader. This woman will use the love and the courage that she has in abundance, to always show you the way to be the finest person you can possibly be. She leads you by her example and her example is always virtuous, wise, patient, and powerful. You will not want to mess with this mother!

A perfect mother is respected; she is so respected, you want to behave out of respect for her.

A perfect mother is always wise. She always knows the right thing to do in any situation and she knows her children better than they know themselves. She can balance her marriage, her life, her work, her children and all the dramas that come up each day.

A perfect mother is powerful. She makes things happen; you may not know how she does it, but she can do anything from inspiring you to learn your multiplication tables, to making a Dorothy or Tin Man costume on 24 hours notice. She also knows how to work with the school system so that somehow even situations with bad teachers work out.

A perfect mother understands the need for boundaries and discipline and administers this requirement with the utmost fairness. She does not let you get away with a thing and when she says something, she means it. She follows through with discipline and she keeps her word.

A perfect mother is a healer of everything from broken hearts and shredded feelings, to banged-up heads and scraped knees. She can feel what you need and knows just what to say or do to make the situation feel better.

A perfect mother can cook, not just a little, but really create fantastic meals and desserts and best of all, birthday cakes! She understands nutrition and always provides just the right combination of healthy meals, snacks and treats.

A perfect mother takes care of herself by always looking like you can be proud of her, dressing well, doing hair and makeup and being healthy. She does not drink or smoke and she is slim and trim.

A perfect mother is psychic. She can just feel when you need her. She can feel that something is wrong. She hears your thoughts and she just knows.

A perfect mother is accomplished and polished. She can help with homework, manage all the administrative work of running a household, do all the shopping, find bargains, decorate perfectly, have style and poise, and endless energy. She may also have a career outside the home.

A perfect mother shares the wisdom of business politics with her children as well as how to climb the corporate or professional career ladder.

A perfect mother never 'leaves' us. She is always available to us: rain or shine, no matter how tired she may be, she is there.

A perfect mother is an example of compassion, caring and strength of character. She keeps her word and she means what she says.

A perfect mother admits her mistakes and apologizes when she is wrong. This is not an oxymoron. Even perfect mothers make mistakes.

A perfect mother does not allow teasing between and among siblings. She fosters love among all the members of the nuclear and extended family. She reminds her children that they will not be children forever and they will need each other as adults and that the love they establish between themselves today will last a lifetime.

A perfect mother does not have favorites, loving her children equally.

A perfect mother is also a different mother to each of her children based on their individual personalities.

A perfect mother demonstrates how to be a good wife and what a good marriage looks like.

A perfect mother keeps everything in balance, for without balance, families do not work.

A perfect mother uses good judgment all the time.

A perfect mother has future sight, understanding that what happens today will dramatically affect tomorrow and all the tomorrows to come.

A perfect mother is a wonderful teacher, helping you to learn self-esteem, confidence and how to learn from your mistakes without feeling stupid or guilty.

A perfect mother respects your space, your choices and your friends. She welcomes your friends.

A perfect mother balances everything with grace, no matter what has happened to her in her life, whether it is a death, job loss or hardship. She lives her wisdom. However, the reality is that few mothers make it to the category of perfect mothers. Hint: sometimes life happens to them!

## There is No Learning in Perfection

Everyone comes here for the experience that mortal life offers, including the experience of motherhood. Mothers are mortal; they make mistakes, get tired and rue certain days. Sometimes their judgment is cloudy; sometimes they do what their mothers did, even if it was a lousy thing to do.

Mothers are often astonished at how profoundly difficult being a parent actually is and why, for some mothers, no matter what they do, their children do not respect them.

Mothers very often do not only what their mothers did, but also what their lineages of women have done for easily a thousand years. Literally, they perpetuate their generational patterns of parenting. This is true in sexual abuse cases: this is a family secret that just never heals, and that secret is the endless cycle of abuse. These women have no idea how to change the cycle. They know it has to change and they spend lifetimes waiting for someone else to make things better and to rescue them. Sometimes, women like this just really need to look in the mirror and recognize that the face of change they are seeking is looking back at them. Truly, sometimes you just have to rescue yourself.

Some mothers insist that their daughters blindly follow religious tradition, even if that tradition is cruel, abusive and archaic to everyone in general and to women specifically.

Some mothers are afraid of motherhood and some are afraid of their children. Some are terrified that their children will not love them and become incapable of providing balanced discipline or any discipline at all.

Some mothers are in competition with their children, be they male or female. This leads to tremendous feelings of resentment in both directions: the mother resents the child and the child resents the fact that he or she can never please their mother. This inability to please a parent often occurs when the parent can sense or see that their child's ability in a given area, be it music, cooking, writing or just making friends far exceeds the mother's. This causes the mother to find fault with the son or daughter. This constant criticism acts like an acid eating away at the child and the relationship between mother and child. It will always be contentious unless the mother chooses to change how she views her child's inherent abilities.

Some mothers are so immature that they never see how smart their children are and that their children are running intellectual circles around them.

Some mothers detest motherhood and they make sure their children know it. They create guilt in their children so that their children spend endless amounts of useless time trying to make them happy, which, for this type of mother, is truly the impossible dream.

On-the-job training is normally the rule for most women and even most really smart women feel overwhelmed by a first baby. For others, the second child pushes them to the brink of insanity. Other women manage elegantly with ten children. Those ladies learned the true meaning of the word delegate responsibility to the older children!

## The Artificial Pedestal

Mothers are mortal, get tired, make mistakes and forget that they are on an artificial pedestal that no one can ever really achieve. Every mother has a spiritual philosophy of what a perfect mother is and often they privately believe that they are inadequate. They suffer with this concept for a very long time.

We have all placed our mothers or our concept of motherhood on an artificial pedestal. Pedestals are cold and lonely places. No one really remembers asking to be placed there and virtually all moms would like to be able to climb down and join the ranks of merely mortal souls who do their best each day.

Death happens in families all over the world. Even an outstanding mother may falter, fall and feel crushed under the weight of grief at the personal loss of a family member. In some cases, she may not be allowed to grieve, but may be expected to keep the rest of the family going. Here again being on that pedestal of expected perfected wisdom will make healing that mother's grief agonizing. Every mother deserves to be allowed to grieve in her own way, without the artificial mantle of unrealistic expectation.

Most women who become mothers either biologically, through marriage, and/or adoption have no idea what they are getting themselves into! Thank goodness! If any of them knew how really challenging motherhood is, many would opt out for another type of life. However, they do not know. They cannot see the future and that is just as well.

It would be wonderful to say that all mothers love, but even that is not true. Most mothers learn to love not just their children, but the lives created by having children. Once you have a child, you become a different person because circumstances demand it. You do not have a choice. If you stay the same, then something is terribly wrong.

If a woman hates motherhood or never makes the transition into this new identity, then part of her will be miserable for the rest of her life and she will share her misery with most people she meets. She will make her family life nightmarish.

Often a woman will note that she 'did the best she could in her situation.' The truth is that when she says that, part of her is thinking deep inside that there may have been better ways for her to have handled many life situations. Other women who feel confident about their mothering experience will believe in themselves and note that they have done an excellent job and they are proud of themselves.

Ultimately, every woman has a spiritual philosophy about what a perfect mother is but not every woman believes she can ever come close to living up to that level of excellence or deserves to be on that artificial pedestal of motherhood expectation. How each woman meets the challenge of being a mother, of living up to that spiritual philosophy, will ultimately define her spiritual path for this lifetime and all her lifetimes to come. Her children will also define the motherhood spiritual philosophy by what they found in her. The cycle continues. Ultimately, it is the extraordinarily courageous woman who chooses to follow the path of maternal enlightenment and learn how to be the best mother she can possibly be.

## The Karmic Opportunity

Analyze your own mother's performance not as judgment, but as teacher – and take her off that pedestal!

Our parents are our greatest teachers. What did your mother teach you?

If she were kind, you would have learned kindness.

If she were cruel, you would have learned that we each have a choice in how to behave and her choice was painful for you. Now you can make a different choice because of what you learned from her.

The more valuable you can view your experience with your mother, the more you can learn from her without bitterness or resentment.

If you can accept these lessons, you may be able to forgive her and see her differently.

This process can heal you and your relationship with her or with your own children.

## Prayer

Dear Lord, please show me the ways of Divine Wisdom in my job of being a mother. Help me to hear my children on a spiritual level and to respond with sensitivity and wisdom. Amen.

The Lightworker's Guide to

## Week 21    Flowers

What is it about flowers that make them so very magical? Why do we give flowers on so many occasions? We give flowers because flowers emit a very high frequency of goodness, light and healing.

Flowers in a hospital room soften the shock of why someone is there in the first place. Flowers for a new mother in or out of a hospital celebrate the birth of new life.

Flowers at a funeral also soften the harsh reality of why everyone has gathered. After people have left, those same flowers offer a certain level of comfort that there is still something beautiful in the world despite the darkness they may be feeling in their grief.

Flowers at birthdays celebrate the life someone is living.

Flowers on Valentine's Day honor the passion of love in an amazing myriad of colors. No guy goes wrong giving flowers on this day. Many people who receive flowers, given on special days, cherish those memories by pressing those fragile petals between pages of romantic books. The symbol of flowers is so great and the sentiment of a special love so precious that preserving the petals seems to preserve the memories as well.

Flowers on Mother's or Father's Day are also wonderful sentiments, providing an offering of beauty as a happy memory.

However, not everyone thinks that flowers are worth giving. Why give flowers? They will ultimately die and you will have wasted the money on them, they say, full of righteous confidence. But righteous confidence would be wrong here because everything dies, everything changes and without the opportunity to experience those precious moments of beauty, we are all diminished. If someone you love loves flowers, even if you think they are a 'waste of money,' give them gorgeous flowers anyway! The recipient will feel honored, special and noticed and you will be enhanced as a person for having done it.

Flowers were put here for a reason, actually for thousands of reasons, but for this discourse, they are here to brighten your day, splash your world with color and lift your spirits. Flowers have so many jobs to do! If a house is profoundly negative, flowers will die quickly. The longer the flowers live, the more positive the house. Flowers are such a sensitivity barometer!

Sometimes someone will give another person flowers 'just because.' 'Just because' flowers are the best because it meant that the giver had to think really happy thoughts about the recipient and then put those happy/loving thoughts into floral action. Without exception, the recipient will smile and feel a sudden sense of love toward the giver. Did you ever notice that the recipient just tells everyone that their special someone or their friend gave them these flowers? It is as if they are saying, 'see, I am really special because someone thought of me with the beauty of these flowers!'

It is always acceptable to give yourself flowers, to have them around and to find a satisfaction in them. Have flowers on your desk all the time if you can, even a single rose or carnation will brighten an office and ease the conversations taking place there, almost as if people do not want to harm the flowers with harsh words.

How amazing it is to live in a world with so many gorgeous flowers! Flowers, much like love, are glorious gifts from God, available to everyone, at all times.

## The Karmic Opportunity

Open your heart and give someone flowers 'just because.' It is the kindness and generosity you will want for yourself.

Give yourself flowers because you are just that special. Your subconscious will be absolutely delighted!

## Prayer

Heavenly Father, thank you with all my heart for the beauty and glory of flowers. I send love and gratitude to the Earth for providing such gorgeous magnificence in my life. Amen.

# Everyday Karma

## Week 22    Processing Catastrophic News: Creating Karmic Balance

Every single day there is news of a catastrophe: a ship sinks, houses burn down, or there is a hurricane that wipes out whole regions. We hear about people who are murdered or who die suddenly of a thousand different things. There are crane, train and plane catastrophes as well. Then there are sudden accidents, divorces, job losses, terrible economic news, and changes in life situations, kidnappings and child abuse cases. In an instant, lives are forever altered.

Military people in war are feeling greater and greater levels of stress. Is it possible that their stress is not just their location alone, but their connection to the volume of events happening at home as well?

How do we as human beings begin to process not just each individual case, but the sheer volume of astounding, heart-wrenching information day after day?

How do we, as caring souls, offer compassion from our internal well, without wondering, sometimes, if that well is becoming dry?

How do we balance the sadness with happiness? If something bad happens to us personally, how do we ever feel that we can be happy again?

It used to be that only caregivers and professionals in certain fields had to face these sad things day after day. That is no longer the case. With the Internet and other instantaneous methods of communication, we are now no more than a moment away from being horrified, astounded and/or outraged.

One of the elements to all of this is the concept of being connected, psychically, with all that is happening. The Hawaiian Huna tradition explains that we are connected to everything we have ever seen, touched or been a part of as well as everyone we have ever met and every place we have ever been, through something called 'aka' cords. Aka cords are thin blue strands of energy that emanate out from our solar plexus, just beneath the breastbone. The more we are electronically connected with people, places and things, the more we are energetically and psychically connected as well. Literally, we are all becoming more and more linked to the tragedies and the catastrophes that we see. All of these things are affecting everyone on the planet, whether they want to be connected to them or not. Perhaps that concept of five degrees of separation is now reduced to a threadbare three or four. What we will eventually realize is that, to maintain our emotional well being, we have to maintain something called karmic balance.

So, how does it work, this concept called karmic balance? How can we bring meaning to what appears to be senseless death, bizarre violence or nature's fury?

We find balance by focusing on things that already exist in our lives for which we can be happy about and/or grateful.

We can also focus on truly enjoying the moment we are in because each of these wonderful moments will eventually become precious memories.

We must also learn to practice detached compassion by sending prayer without attaching to the emotion of the situation. This goes a very long way in helping all of us to maintain mental balance.

Ultimately, however, we need to remember that karma is always fair and that just because we cannot see the big picture regarding this tsunami, plane crash or murder, does not mean that it does not exist. We never know what karma any type of death or destruction is satisfying, group karmic disaster rebalancing, or what lessons there are for all the players to learn. Perspective, non-judgment and patience can get us through the roller coaster of emotions many of us are seeing each day.

As painfully hard as it frequently is, step back from any of these events and look for the obvious and the peripheral lessons everyone is going to learn. If there were no lessons to be learned, then human beings would not have any of these experiences in the first place. We are here for experiences and often these poignantly precious lessons are powerful karmic balancers. In the schoolhouse that is mortal life on Earth there are many degrees of experience to acquire. Karma has a tremendous responsibility to provide all of them to us throughout all of the lives we will eventually live, including the really hard ones. The more fully we embrace each experience, learn each lesson and then grow, the fewer difficult experiences we will see repeated in our lives. It is this perspective that will ultimately enable us to observe what is happening around us, with a greater degree of wisdom and compassion.

## The Karmic Opportunity

Remember to practice detached compassion: send love without attaching to the emotion of the situation.

Each national/international catastrophe is a powerful opportunity to send love and healing, to flex your spiritual muscle.

Request that angels be sent to rescue crews, medical personnel and on-scene investigators to help them deal with the staggering level of losses people are suffering.

It takes courage to provide service in the face of another's loss, but that courage will be profoundly appreciated.

## Prayer

Dear God above, please help me to understand the ways of perfect karmic balance. Guide me, Father, in understanding the lessons from all that I am seeing and experiencing. Thank you God, for always being by my side and in my life. I know that no matter what I am experiencing, you are there for me. Amen.

## Week 23  The Ego of Self-Degradation: Poor Me!

How can ego be associated with self-degradation? Because ego is how we perceive ourselves, we are often led to believe that ego is arrogance -- which it can be, but it can also be one of Poor Me. Both views take lots of energy to maintain, usually other people's energy.

Some people are told from childhood that something about them is either unworthy or unlovable. The subconscious of a child absolutely believes what the parent says, so the child's self esteem is then chronically depleted because constant criticism acts like an energy drain. Without the energy of positive thought and positive belief, children and, ultimately adults do not have the energy to move forward with the enjoyment of living life.

This negative environment may also cause the person to feel that there will never be enough for them and some people develop a sense of inner jealously because of this. Jealously is fear with a grasping face. People who are endlessly jealous are terrified that there will not be enough love, energy, and attention for them.

Eventually, a reality of ego is created that the person is not good, smart, wealthy, pretty or capable enough to do or be anything. The person's subconscious perpetuates that view. Poor me, they think, I can never escape this negative belief in myself. Everyone else is better than I am and has more than I do!

As adults, Poor Me personalities seem to stay in that endless cycle of neediness that can literally take energy from everyone around them. Not only do they feel that there is not enough for them, they also feel a jealously for what other people have achieved. Often they become energy vampires, taking far more emotional energy than people meant to offer them.

It takes self-awareness to uncover this pattern and then to choose to break this cycle. We really are much better at everything than we think. Putting ourselves down may seem fashionable, but it is extremely detrimental. We can each be terrific at whatever we choose. We are each lovable in a myriad of ways. We can each stop feeling the Poor Me energy and start to give and then watch what tremendous gifts can ultimately be received.

A Poor Me personality feels as if they have nothing to give. The reality is that we all have a tremendous amount to give to others, even if it is just our smile and a kind word. What we give out can come back 1000 fold in tremendously positive ways. We just have to choose that path.

One important aspect of choosing a different path is to recognize that we cannot change anyone else: we can only change ourselves. We can sincerely ask for help in this transformation. It will require courage and insight. When we ask for a teacher to show us a gentle path to wholeness -- one will be provided.

We must believe in ourselves. Ultimately, this will turn out to be one more important experience on our path to enlightenment.

## The Karmic Opportunity

If you are a 'poor me' personality, choose to change and be a more positive personality. Self-perceptions can be changed with concentrated and often assisted effort.

If you are with a 'poor me' personality and this person refuses to change, you have to decide if the karmic lesson is one of establishing your identity and leaving this person.

Sometimes you are with a person who forces you to look at what you really want in life and if you are not finding it, to decide to make a more positive change.

Staying with someone who consistently drains you creates subtle, simmering anger that begins to destroy you from the inside out.

The karmic opportunity is honest evaluation of what is the greatest good for all concerned.

## Affirmation

I am a wise person who always seeks the greatest good in each situation.

I have the ability to change my past perceptions about myself.

There is a tremendous abundance in the Universe and it is available to me at all times.

## Prayer

Dear Lord, please grant me the wisdom to know the best course of action in my current situation. Please assist me in finding help to move forward with the life I am living. Amen.

## Week 24    Fathers

Parenting has often been discussed. What it means to be a mother seems to be more universally understood than what it means to be a father. There are far more "how to" books for mothering than for fathering, as if somehow, fathering is not quite as important.

Each of us has our own definition of what a father is or is not supposed to be based on our own unique experience. In today's world, intact families are the unusual anomaly, no longer the norm. My daughter once remarked that she was the only one among her friends with original parents in a healthy marriage.

Is this state of affairs of separated families a good or a bad thing? It is not good or bad; that's just how it is now. Often, because it seems that karma is being speeded up, many things have to be resolved in this lifetime regarding relationships and at a much greater speed than in the past. What that means is that couples lead more complicated lives and it is often not as easy or as time affordable to work things out between couples. This, in turn, means that there are more and more families without fathers. Sometimes it seems that there is more karma being created on the negative side in divorces than can be resolved in one lifetime. It does not have to be that way.

Some divorce situations are so filled with rage and anger that kids feel disloyal if they try to maintain their love for both parents. Some parents use their kids as pawns to punish their partners. No one ever wins this pissing contest: everyone just gets really stinky.

Perhaps the greatest loss to families is the concept of the involved father. The involved father is a man who helps as an equal partner, respects the mother and remains in an active partnership with the mother, providing balanced discipline for the kids. Parents who support one another are often quite rare.

Many women who grow up without fathers never really understand men and often take on their mother's hatred of men, which then deprives the daughter of a loving relationship with a good husband. Many boys grow up with fathers who hate and abuse women and the same situation is the result. These things work both ways.

We need fathers. The reason we have two parents is the balance and wisdom a child receives from both a male and female perspectives.

We need fathers to be teachers to their kids, to be examples of what moral values stand for and for teaching that kindness backed with strength of character are the foundations for a successful life. We need fathers who keep their word and are fair in all their dealings.

The problem is that men and women who did not have positive role models often have no idea how to be that kind of parent. They fumble and seldom ask for help. Often they say well, it was ok for me, why is not it ok for my child? It simply is not. Each of us has to do a better job of parenting than was done for us and if we had great parenting, build on that foundation. Perhaps it is a good idea to identify what good fathers bring to the family.

A really good Dad is a teacher for all his children, offering them the benefit of his wisdom when it comes to people, politics, career guidance, sportsmanship, building things, tools, and life in general.

The father who just sits in front of the TV and never spends time reading or holding his little kids misses out on an incredible opportunity to teach his children something. When you patiently teach them, it means you are spending time with them. One of my sons noted that some of his happiest times were when he was in the garage working on something with his dad - the give and take, the patience of learning how tools work. There were the times when they built gigantic Lego projects together and the guidance received at those times, enabled our son had to build complicated Lego models on his own as a practice for following written directions.

Fathers teach balance in a marriage: doing chores, washing dishes, sharing in the cleaning, yard work and errand running.

Fathers teach consideration when shopping for birthdays, Mother's Day and holidays for mothers and siblings.

Fathers teach politics when they discuss their jobs with their sons and daughters so that the children can understand how the real world functions from a man's perspective.

Children learn what marriage is like only from watching their parents. Kids will do what their parents do unless they are very, very savvy and can differentiate from what was great about their parent's marriage and what required improvement.

Boys learn how to treat women with respect by watching their father interact with their mother. If the father is kind and considerate, then sons learn this. Girls learn how women are to be treated from their father's attitude toward their mother. The abusive/disrespectful father creates abusive kids, abusive adults, and ultimately abusive parents. The physically and verbally violent father creates horrific trauma for children literally for generations to come.

It is always better to have a single mother family than have a violent family with an abusive father. The kids never really forgive the mother for continuing to allow the abuse much less the father for abusing all of them. Why didn't she just leave him, they ask themselves for the rest of their lives, until they end up in the same type of marriage. It takes quite a bit of courage to leave that life.

Fathers are incredibly valuable and families need fathers for love and for balance. Families do not need fathers who are never there or who abuse.

Like everything else in human relationships, the father connection is very complicated. Let us hope that more men decide to be really great fathers because they are incredibly important in everyone's life.

So, on Father's Day or any day of the year, let us honor all those who do represent the best of fathering and let us say a prayer for all those fathers who do not, in the hopes that some day, they may come to understand the tremendous importance of the father's role in a child's life.

## The Karmic Opportunity

If you do not know how to be a great dad, then decide to learn how to become one.

Look around you and see who has successful relationships with his children and then seek his advice on how you can create a positive nurturing relationship with your own children.

Make your relationship with your children a top priority.

Spend time with your children: be patient and listen.

Do not automatically say no when they ask you something.

### Affirmation

I vow to be a better dad to my children than my father was to me.

I love spending time with my children and they love spending time with me.

## Prayer

Dear Lord, help me to find the pathway to being an outstanding dad to my children. Guide me in the ways of wisdom and love. Thank you God for showing me the ways of building a happy life with my family. Amen.

The Lightworker's Guide to

## Week 25   Parking Spaces

Life is hard. Life is a whole lot harder when you are in a hurry and cannot find a parking space. Perhaps that has never happened to you, but if it has, it can absolutely ruin your day.

Most of the time you are on a time schedule and not finding parking just seems to make things really difficult. When you are in that endless parking structure during a busy time and the whole world seems to be shopping, going to the airport, leaving you no place to park - what a nightmare that can be! Perhaps you begin to feel yourself getting really angry. Perhaps you are angry with yourself for not allowing enough time to find a spot. During the holidays, at certain malls, it can take an employee an hour to find a place to put their car.

What can you do to make finding a parking space easier? This is a karmic issue because finding parking is like finding wealth. If there is never a space for you, it almost feels like there is never wealth for you either. Everyone else gets there first and there is nothing left for you. These feelings come very close to envy and anger when you see someone else just slide right into that space that should have been yours! Somehow a flash of anger just pops up. Some people actually swear at the situation.

This is not a good thing because it makes anything that happens when you finally get out of the car less enjoyable.

So, what is a person to do about this feeling, this worry about parking and its follow-on concept of finding wealth? Be happy for that person who just slides into that space. Do not envy them; be happy for them. This means that you are telling your subconscious that you are thinking generously, that you are not angry and that in life there really is plenty for all of us. This also fully embraces the concept that you are confident that there will be a spot for you. Confidence is needed here, not anger. You will manifest what you fear the most. Do not be afraid of not finding a spot, of not finding wealth.

Metaphysics teaches that there is an unlimited supply in the Universe. Billionaires have surely proven that by making an astonishing amount of money. That opportunity is available to anyone with the karmic courage, desire, smarts and energy to make it happen. OK, so being a mega-millionaire may not be your karmic path, but wealth - as you define it - can be.

Let us return to the subject of parking. This is the karmic concept of creating a reality. People eventually will tell you that you are just lucky when it comes to parking, but you will know the truth: that parking, like anything else, is how you perceive it - wealth or lack. You decide.

What is one to do in a hurry when you really need that spot to manifest? Follow the simple, easy steps in The Karmic Opportunity (right below) for creating parking karma.

So, karmically, every time you congratulate someone for finding a spot - perhaps even a spot you wanted, - you are sending out wonderful energy. This also holds true for congratulating someone when they get promoted, find a good job, or win the lottery. What you send out comes back to you, and that return just may be anything from a pay raise, to a perfect shady spot to park on a hot day, or very close to the entrance on a rainy day. Karma is always operating. The law is always in force. Now, look forward to a better parking experience and possibly more wealth in the future!

## The Karmic Opportunity

Ask your subconscious before you leave to find a parking spot for you right near the entrance to your location.

As you are driving there, ask once or twice while on the road.

When you get to the parking area and you notice someone find a great spot, say to yourself Good for them - see there is plenty for them and plenty for me - a great spot is just waiting for me!

When the spot manifests, thank your subconscious for finding the spot (give your subconscious a name you like so you can create a great relationship with him or her) gratitude will ensure that the same thing will happen in the future.

Enjoy the moment of pulling into the spot: see, there is plenty out there.

Print out these directions and tape them to your dash so that this can become a habit until the concept of manifesting wonderful parking just lives within you.

**Affirmation**

I always find the perfect place to park.

I know that there is always plenty for me whether it is parking or wealth!

The Lightworker's Guide to

## Week 26   The Relentless Pursuit of Perfection

Lots of people these days seem to be seeking perfection. They want to have perfect houses, perfect cars, a perfect face and body, perfect spouses and of course, the ultimate must have: perfect children!

Everything must be decorated perfectly, all grades must be A+ and everything must be in perfect order. The pursuit of perfection often extends to being very afraid of what other people will think if something happens or is said that is not somehow perfect.

"The Relentless Pursuit of Perfection" is a great motto for a Lexus, but it is a not a great goal for a human being. Why? Because human beings are here to experience things and to learn about all the facets of love and fear: a better motto would be the Relentless Pursuit of Wisdom. If you were already perfect on a soul evolution level, you would not even be here at all. Often times, you spend so much time trying to be perfect that you forget you are here to gain wisdom. If you live an utterly perfect life, then you focus on the minutia of life and miss the big picture.

You see this in parents who endlessly schedule every spare minute of their children's time. Never an extra moment to just be idle or have quiet or creative play time. No, every minute must be "perfectly" occupied. Even weekends offer no rest to just ponder life with schedules so tight that the goal of a perfect day becomes one of getting everything done, no matter how tired, irritable, or stressed it makes everyone else.

Perfection extends into relationships, where both men and women have utterly unrealistic expectations of mates. While you may know for sure that you are not perfect, you absolutely want your mate, or boy/girlfriend to be perfect: have a perfect body, a perfect clothes sense and be a perfect family. You also want this partner to always know the perfect words to say in any situation, be politically savvy to your every need and never have a bad day. Oh, and you want them to be appropriately romantic and sense when you want romance, and more importantly, when you do not. You are also in a tremendous hurry to be perfect and you want it yesterday!

Not too realistic is it?

Now fast forward to the end of your life, when all the clauses of your life contract are up and you return home to the Heaven World. But first your soul gets to listen to what those around you think of you when you die. You will be able to hear what other people who are still living, have to say about you. You will hear their view of how you led your life.

It would be wise to think about this now, not wait until the end. At the end of the day, at the end of your life, people will not remember that you were perfect. They will remember whether or not you were kind and loving. Most of all, they will feel that they really miss you because the strength of your presence brought hope and help. However, most of all your friends and your family will remember that you balanced your strength with kindness and the tremendous power of a loving heart with wisdom.

## The Karmic Opportunity

The karmic opportunity here is to pray that at the end of your life, hopefully people will remember whether or not:

You were kind to others.

You took time to listen, even when you were tired or rushed or did not know what to say.

When you listened, you really heard the person.

You were patient, again, even if you were tired, or rushed.

You cared more about service than power.

You were wise about situations.

You understood that true politics is more about wisdom than manipulation.

You looked at each situation and worked toward the greater good.

You were good to yourself.

You were aware of the power of your words to heal, hurt or inspire.

You sacrificed when it was appropriate, but not out of martyrdom.

You were a good friend or neighbor.

You were a person of courage.

You were a good spouse.

You were a good sibling.

You were a good son or daughter.

You were an honest person.

You thought of the feelings of others and choose your words with kindness.

You loved with all your heart.

You openly and physically embraced others.

You were always generous and caring, generous with money, time, food and ideas.

You were not egotistical.

# Everyday Karma

**Affirmations**

I have plenty of time to rest and relax.

My house, life and family do not have to be perfect.

Happiness is more important than perfection.

I always seek the greatest wisdom in any situation.

The Lightworker's Guide to

## Week 27   The Acceleration of Time

The following is a theory about time to ponder.

Everyone you talk to these days seems busier than ever. We are just a profoundly busy bunch of people. But this busyness is not making anyone happy, or giving anyone a feeling of being fulfilled. You do not necessarily feel that you are accomplishing more or getting more done. Rather, this sense of having so much to do is creating a subtle growing feeling of being overwhelmed. It is as if somehow time has been accelerated. It feels as if there is so much to do each day and less time with which to get it done.

Is this possible? Is it possible for time to be accelerated? Yes, it is actually possible for the perception of time acceleration to have taken place. Science has documented the fact that, with the Sumatran earthquake of December 26, 2004 and the resulting tsunami, the echo of that quake and the staggering sloshing of water felt around the planet three times slightly shifted the earth's rotation. This massive earth change also caused the rotation of the earth to accelerate by certain fractions of a second. Again, that earth rotation acceleration may not seem as if it would even be noticeable to anyone, but the scientific fact is that there is a tiny, tiny increase in the rapidity with which this earth rotates.

Which means that time is going ever so slightly faster.

Do imperceptible changes affect things? The answer to this question goes back to the scientific study of the temperature of the world's oceans. Oceanographers know that even a fraction of a degree shift in seawater temperature has a ripple effect throughout the entire ocean ecosystem. This temperature shift can affect breeding, behavior, migration patterns and weather patterns. How can something so small have such an effect? Because when the balance of the sea experiences a change, that change has to echo throughout the seas. The oceans have to figure out how to bring themselves back into balance. This is a planet-wide phenomenon because all the oceans of the world, all the seas, all the skies and all the air are connected. Nothing operates in isolation. Everything that is done affects something else in some small way. This means that even a small change in ocean temperature will affect the entire planet.

If that is true, then a tiny, tiny increase in the acceleration of the rotation of the planet can create an acceleration in time. So, when the massive 800-mile thrusting up of the plates off Sumatra created a colossal sloshing of the planet's oceans, this change echoed out to affect the planet itself, its very rotation.

If this is possible, then perhaps the best way for you to deal with that feeling that you have less time is to understand that the earth has changed. You have to find new ways to adjust, to rebalance yourself as the earth is rebalancing itself after that massive quake.

This situation is not good or bad, it just is. So how do you go about rebalancing after such a life-changing event? First you come to understand that you are not crazy. The feeling that there is less time is accurate. Now that you know this, you can decide individually how you will adjust to it, just like sea creatures have to adjust to a change in ocean temperature.

It is as if a limitation has been imposed, subtle, but definitely perceptible. So to accommodate this limitation, you may have to decide to reprioritize what is really important to you, what is important for you to spend time on. Perhaps that is why this happened in the first place. Maybe you just did not realize that some priorities have to change and this is nature's way of showing you a new way. Of course, being human, you resist change. But also because you are human, you can choose to change, not fight it and begin to decide to shift – go with a different flow of time. Maybe some things just are not important any more. Maybe your focus is to spend time on what really matters.

The irony in all of this is that, in the long run, this may offer you the sense that you have cleared some things out of the way and have made way for something new. You have streamlined time for yourself. Perhaps, in the long run, you may decide that this really will have happened for your greater good.

## The Karmic Opportunity

Now is the time to embrace slowing down just a little bit, and allowing yourself to have more rest.

The more rested you are, the more you will seem to be able to accomplish.

Accept that there is only so much that can get done in one day. Let that be all right and not a fault.

Decide what is really important in life and allow yourself to focus on that.

## Affirmations

There is always plenty of time to get everything done.

I wisely focus on what is the most important to me.

I love the life I am living and the people in it.

The Lightworker's Guide to

## Week 28   Why Don't Psychics Win the Lottery?

Did you ever wonder why psychics don't pick winning lottery numbers?

Did you ever wonder why psychics don't accurately predict earthquakes with exact time and dates, or where hurricanes are going to make landfall or that there will be a fire at a specific time and place? How about pinpointing the path of a tornado - wouldn't that be helpful to predict accurately?

Did you ever wonder why psychics don't accurately predict personal events in their own future: like the exact time and date when their children will be born or when they will find their mate or where that new job will come from?

Why can't psychics predict when, exactly, a relative will die, especially someone close to them if it is an accident or an illness or a sudden death?

What about those psychics who predicted that California would fall into the Pacific way back in the 1970s?

Why were they wrong - or were they?

Why can't psychics predict what we want them to predict to make our lives and even their own lives easier?

Because it just doesn't work that way. First of all, we are all psychic - every single one of us. So, now that we have established that we are talking about ourselves that pretty much levels the playing field. At some point in our lives, we have all had psychic experiences about something and we were correct about what we felt. The problem is that we are not psychic all the time and, most of the time, when we do get 'a feeling about something,' we ignore it. We dismiss the very sense that would help us over time.

Just what is a psychic sense? Since we have all felt it, try defining it! Wrap your brain around a dream you had last night that slipped away as you awoke. It is like trying to hold on to a wee bit of mist.

A psychic sense is a feeling, a knowing without specific fact, an inner connection to something communicating with you that you cannot see. It is like tuning an old time radio to find the right frequency to get a clearer signal. You get bits and pieces of what is trying to be communicated, but the signal is often intermittent, so you never get the whole message. You feel lucky to get the gist of the thought. Often it is so fleeting that probably 90% of the time you dismiss it as fantasy.

And, like different frequencies on that radio dial, different frequencies offer different types of psychic information. Sometimes it is a premonition; sometimes it is a feeling about a person. Sometimes it is a sense of timing about a situation that you cannot explain. There are all kinds of psychic senses. Perhaps the most common are the ones that parents have about their children. Sometimes a parent will sense when something is wrong with their child. Psychic information comes in many forms. Sometimes it comes to us in a dream - we just wake up knowing something because it was shown to us in that dream. Other times it comes to us as we surface from sleep - with a message, something we are to do or say to someone. Inspiration is also a form of psychic sense so strong that you have no choice but to record it. Amadeus Mozart was literally bombarded with musical information and it poured out of him: he had no choice but to write it down. Because his music is some of the highest frequency music in the known world, it was obviously divinely inspired. How many writers also note that they just 'had a flash of inspiration' and knew what to write? Consider how many inventors have awakened with details of a groundbreaking invention.

What is psychic information? It is information that will help us in any given situation know the correct path. It can warn us, make us more alert and aware of our surroundings as we go through our day. There is the true story of a lady who had a strong feeling that her sister would be in an accident that day. So she called her sister and warned her about the danger she saw if her sister did in fact run an errand. Her sister assured her that she had no intention of leaving the house that day. However, circumstances and karma being what they are, the sister did in fact run an unexpected errand, and at the very spot where her sister had warned her to be careful, she almost had an accident. However, because she had been made aware of the potential danger, she avoided that accident.

There was the lady who had a recurring dream about an accident her husband would have - with amazing detail, which is unusual in dreams. As each detail in the dream began to come true, she stopped her husband from taking the final action that would have ended in his death.

Sometimes, we are allowed to know something bad is going to happen, but we are not allowed specific details. The theory is that we only have the karma for certain information. We are just not going to get it all at once - which begs the question, why aren't we allowed to get the total picture?

We live mortal life for the experiences it offers, the times when there is both good and bad news. The sudden shock of something (bad as it seems) is an opportunity to see how we react under pressure, so knowing about it in advance will rob us of that specific experience. However, as we progress on our spiritual path, we are allowed to have greater and greater levels of communication with the source of the information about our potential futures. Sometimes we can look at a situation and actually see how it is going to evolve if various action choices are taken. This is spiritual insight. The more we pay attention to this, the wiser will be our choices.

## Communicating with the Higher Realms

So, just how does it work, this communication with the higher realms? This is the essence of the spiritual path - the road less traveled by the majority of us. When we embark on a spiritual path, we learn to connect to our Higher Self. We learn to ask for help from our angels, we learn how to listen to that still small voice within us all. In essence, we learn to trust that which we cannot see, audibly 'hear,' taste or smell. We learn to use our five senses exceptionally well, and then we learn how to use the sixth sense - our psychic sense.

Our psychic sense feels, hears, smells, sees and often tastes things other people cannot (like the taste of fear). This indefinable psychic sense is for us to use for our betterment. The truest psychic sense will always be for our higher good and for the higher good of those around us. This still, small voice will not tell us to do harm to our neighbor or how to wreak vengeance at the office. Those people who seek to do great harm to themselves or others are hearing a still small voice but it is never their Higher Self.

The more sophisticated our knowledge of the spiritual world, the greater our communication with the higher levels of the spiritual world. In other words, the more we understand about the physics of metaphysics, the more we will understand how to foster this communication, and the more we will learn to trust this communication. The greater this level of trust becomes, the more in tune we will feel with our own Higher Self and those wonderful beings in the Higher realms. Eventually we no longer know where we stop and they start; the wonderful thing is that it no longer matters. Ego leaves us. Does it matter where our inspiration comes from? Is credit for something that important when true creativity is simply divine inspiration anyway? The more that this knowledge lives within us, the more we can trust what we hear.

As we become more psychically in tune with those Higher realms we start to seek quiet, peacefulness, and freedom from the 'noise' of electro-smog, that we can have a clearer link to hearing that still small voice.

How does it feel to hold a butterfly? Feel its little feet? Can we feel the wind on our faces when it flies away? No, we can't, but we know the creature was there because we saw it. A psychic sense is similar to this feeling of holding a butterfly, because both are delicate and almost fragile. Psychically, we know the feeling is there because we begin to sense it and we learn to trust it.

The question becomes why don't we feel that psychic sense 24/7? Mortal life is just too distracting: there is grocery shopping to do, meals to prepare, office politics to analyze, kids to tend to, spouses, friends and family to help. Our plates are constantly full with living day to day. We don't get to sit quietly on a mountaintop and meditate waiting for divine inspiration.

Yet, even with overflowing plates of things to do, we would still be wise to find some quiet time to ourselves to establish that link to the Divine. The Higher Self/Divine connection wants to be sure that we can discern their concepts from our own, so their information feed is done with specific care. When we become more finely in tune to our higher realm connection, we can feel confident in our ability to hear/sense/know the wisdom that can come. Even then, communication is seldom 24/7. Human beings have to have time to assimilate their daily experiences and events. And we humans also have to have time to process the psychic/spiritual information received.

There is a flip side to all of this. Not only do we have to trust the information that we receive, the other side has to trust us with the information they give us. They are showing us a tiny, tiny view of the future. How will we use this information? Will we abuse it? Can we be trusted?

Now, why is the Divine showing us anything? Because as we progress on this path, the goal is to open us up to all that is. To do that, we have to learn to trust what we hear. This is the hardest thing for any mortal to do. Some of the things we think we hear may be challenging to know. How will we handle the information? The more psychic ability we develop, the more spiritual responsibility we acquire in the process. Ultimately, our goal will be to become wise in how we handle all information whether or not it is ordinary or psychic.

## Karma and the Psychic Sense

Some people are using a psychic sense when they pick the lottery numbers and they win the lottery. That person thinks their pick was 'random.' But nothing is random. Everything is connected to a much larger picture. Winning the lottery is karma returning to that person all at once. Think about it. If we were tremendously generous in another life, that generosity has to be returned to us. How it is returned is a very complicated process beyond what most of us can understand, but whatever we do comes back to us, and so it is with the lottery.

The key is how the lottery winner handles the win. How does he or she deal with this new experience of karmic return on previous, past life investment? That is the test. Every karmic opportunity is a learning experience whether it is poverty or great wealth. Most people who win the lottery never consider themselves psychic - just lucky.

What about the psychic who cannot predict that her child, husband, niece, nephew, boss or parent will suddenly die? Is she a bad psychic? It is not whether or not she is a good or bad psychic as much as it is whether or not she is spiritually supposed to know it. If a psychic knows of an impending death, she would naturally try to stop it. If she does not know it is coming, then there is nothing she can do and the karmic path goes on unimpeded.

What if we are afforded the opportunity to see the future death of someone and we can stop it because it is not that person's time to die? In that case we are given the tools to do so and we are expected to use them within reasonable limits.

No one gets it right 100% of the time. Even excellent psychics with a respectable track record see things and yet somehow something changes and what they thought they saw does not happen. Does this mean the person was wrong? No, things do change. It is not personal and the psychic will get the sense that the danger or situation has shifted.

How do we know that what we hear is true? This is such an important question and one of the hardest to answer. There was a case of the mother who was told that her newborn child had meningitis and was dying. The mother felt deep inside her that this was not true and challenged a team of doctors (as astounding as this was, this same situation happened to both of her children). She actually removed the child (each time) from the hospital and had an outside physician test her child and found that one child had a collapsed lung and, later, the other child had a small throat anomaly and neither child had any evidence of meningitis whatsoever. That mother literally saved her children's lives. How did this mother know to trust her own intuition? How? The mother never wavered in her belief that her children were being diagnosed incorrectly. She believed in herself, and she believed in that 'still small voice.' She was also grateful for that inner voice and even more thankful that she had the karma to hear that 'little voice' at all. Karma offered her an opportunity, and she took it. Perhaps the entire situation was a karmic experience for all the players in that drama.

One of the tools to use in learning to trust what we sense and feel is to be still and to listen. We can turn off the music, connect to nature, and de-clutter our homes so that the look and feel of our surroundings is calm. We can write down what messages, if any, we receive upon awakening. We will need plenty of sleep. We will also need to reduce our stress where we can.

Stress, anxiety, fear, guilt, dread, and fatigue create layers of barriers to hearing Higher Self. We always need to remember our goodness as a person. Remember that, as we begin each day, our intention is to do a good job at whatever it is that we do.

Praying with all our hearts before we go to sleep will automatically connect us to the higher realms and actually protect us in the sleep state. The more we pray, the higher our frequency becomes and the easier it is to hear that still small voice.

It is important to pay attention to what is happening in our sleep state. If a person is waking up at 3am night after night, this may mean that there is tremendous stress going on in his or her life. This person will need to work through this stress and work on getting really nourishing sleep. Doing less before going to bed and relaxing more may mean that we are being kinder to ourselves.

As time goes by, we may begin to notice what it feels like when we begin to sense something. Identify that feeling; become really acquainted with it, then become comfortable with it. Look for it. If we find that we have a problem, we may need to ask our Higher Self and our angels for help. We will then need to listen for their reply. Sometimes their answer may not be what we expect. Trust it. Try it out. Notice the growing confidence in acting on the psychic information received. Patience will enable us to trust the outcomes. Sometimes things just have to have time to work themselves out.

As time goes on, learn to trust that voice at greater and greater levels. We are not only trusting Higher Self we are also trusting ourselves. This is an important milestone in our progress on our spiritual path. It also means that our Higher Self also trusts us with more and more information. Hearing Higher Self gets easier and clearer. Remember that we are only allowed to know what we need to know to get any job done. The seasoned psychic knows and accepts this.

We are all psychic. Some of us just practice the skill of listening to that psychic message more than others. This 'listening skill' is a critical skill for advancement on the spiritual path.

## A Variety of Psychic Experiences

There is a gentleman who is a rocket scientist - he works for the aerospace industry. He is extremely 'left brained' and does not really buy into the whole psychic 'thing.' However, he has a remarkable ability. When he goes with his wife to Las Vegas and walks through the casinos, he 'hears' the slot machines tell him when they are going to go to a win. It is incredible that he can hear anything when the noise of any casino is astounding, but he is right 100% of the time. He is not hearing the noise; he is connecting to the energy system of each machine through the auspices of Higher Self. He wins a respectable amount of money and he leaves. The key with this man is that he is not greedy. He also has a psychic sense about when to quit and he listens to it. He is not banned from any casino and he never brags about what he can do. His humility keeps him winning. Karma has to return to you somehow and this must be some unique karmic payback for him.

Many people are pet psychics. None of them hear the situation with an animal the same way. One lady can tell you the situation surrounding why your cat, for example, pees all over the house, but she cannot talk to the cat and tell him or her to stop peeing. Another pet psychic can talk to the animal and foster communication with owners. Then there is the pet psychic who talks to dead animals and helps their owners with their grief.

There are plant psychics. Lots and lots of us are plant psychics. We can walk into a room and hear a plant tell us it is thirsty or over watered or just plain miserable in that location.

Some people are selectively telepathic. They can hear thoughts in small groups or in one-on-one situations. They can also hear when their Higher Self wants them hear someone so that they can help that person. They are not just extremely adept at reading body language; they hear someone else's thoughts. Some can see the aura around the person as they are hearing their thoughts, which further validates what they are hearing. For them it starts out as hearing parts of sentences unsaid. Then it evolves to answering questions before the person asks them. Sometimes it is so profound you cannot tell whether the person actually said something or you just heard their thoughts. This type of psychic has to be particularly careful in their use of this ability because it can completely unnerve the other person. Usually this ability is acquired when the psychic has achieved an important level of spiritual wisdom and can handle what they hear with care. Also, most telepathic individuals are not allowed to hear all thoughts all the time. Madness would surely set in! They could never go to a mall or a theater - how terrible that would be! They hear what they need to hear to do their job.

As mentioned in Week 10, some of the best mechanics are psychic, literally becoming in resonance with the cars they are working on. Most of them would not want to be able to do it all the time - it would be like telepathy, with so many cars on the road, or cars in a parking lot, you would surely become overwhelmed, but the cars you need to hear, you can.

A handful of people have a medical psychic/intuitive ability, which means that they can see into people's bodies and sense the medical anomalies that exist. There are varying degrees of ability for this skill and, the more a person uses it, like any psychic sense, the greater skill he or she can develop. The wise medical psychic/intuitive does not run around telling people what they sense or see. They are judicious and wise in how they use this skill.

Some people see the future - but only glimpses of it. One wife saw her husband taking a trip and that something bad would happen to him. She could not see what bad thing would happen, but she knew that he would not die, and just as she had foreseen, an unfortunate event did happen. The very next trip he made, she again saw that something wonderful would happen to him and it did: he received a medal for his heroic efforts. Why did she see these things? She does not know to this day why - perhaps, just because.

Some people are born knowing how to do remote viewing. In remote viewing, the psychic can literally project their consciousness to any location on the planet and see what is happening there, on the etheric level. Here, again, there are varying levels of this ability as well. While some aspects can be taught, other aspects are extremely specialized such as remote healing. Even here, the remote viewer who is either sending healing or clearing homes can only do what they are karmically allowed to do. If someone is dying, they cannot force that person to live. If they are clearing a house of dark intelligences or ghosts, again, they can only clear what they are karmically allowed to see.

Psychic ability comes to all of us - there are no gifts here – only abilities. The more we use an ability, learn about it, and study all the physics that accompany it, the more we can enhance that ability. However, a little knowledge can be a very dangerous thing. Approaching the more sophisticated skills can be very challenging, such as any type of healing or seeing into the future. If someone becomes aware of their abilities growing, they need to be extremely judicious in their use, especially if it involves other people. He or she must always seek wisdom first. The entire lesson here is the wise use of any ability. Above all, control ego: a person must not brag about what he or she can do. Sharing an amazing experience is one thing, bragging about an ability to heal everyone is arrogant.

Why don't psychics win the lottery? Well, actually, sometimes they do win the lottery but only when they are karmically allowed to do so. Ultimately the growth of psychic ability is a significant step forward in spiritual wisdom.

## The Karmic Opportunity

Everyone is psychic but those who seek to develop this ability carry a larger karmic responsibility:

literally, once you understand how the spiritual world works, you are responsible for the just use of your skill.

Focusing on a constant meditation, staying in that place of frequent unselfish prayer and service will greatly enable you to develop psychic ability.

The more service you perform, the more likely you are to hear your Higher Self.

Trust the times that you can hear that still small voice of Higher Self.

Be humble with the ability that you do receive. Your ability comes from the Divine, release any ego.

## Affirmations

Day by day in every way I am becoming more connected to the Divine.

My ability to hear the still small voice of God is growing in proportion to my growing wisdom.

Love is the guide that allows me to use any psychic ability that I may acquire.

## Prayer

Heavenly Father, I pray for your guidance as I learn how to hear your voice, as I learn how to use divine knowledge to be of greater service to my fellow human beings. Amen.

The Lightworker's Guide to

## Week 29   Friendship

There is a beloved movie from the 1930s where the hero seeks to learn some of the many lessons of love. Literally, he is seeking to find the nature of his own heart. Finally, a wise man explains to him that in the end, it is not so much about how much any one man loves, but about how much one man is loved by others along the path of his life. What a remarkable concept! This is truly the essence of love. This is also the very essence of friendship.

Friendship is not necessarily convenient - people catch you, need you when you have no makeup on and you are busy. They need you to help them anyway.

Friendship is not for the impatient, for your friends deserve your patience, your non-judgmental, kindly, sympathetic listening ear. Your friends do not necessarily need you to solve their problems nor do you need them to solve yours, you each need someone to be there for you.

Friendship is remembering the little things, not just birthdays, but that you borrowed something and you paid it back because it was important to you to keep the relationship in balance. It is also remembering the stresses the person is under when they seem short with you. You will want that same consideration in return.

Friendship is reaching out to start a friendship, being sensitive to the needs of the other person. Friendship is extending yourself for that person.

Friendship is also feeling that you can call someone and they will take time for you. Your friend knows you well enough to understand inherently what you may require in that moment.

One of the critical elements of friendship is never judging the situation of another. If a person is really toxic for you, then maintaining a distance may be better for both of you. But if that person is merely going through a hard time, do not judge - be the best friend you can be in the moment. If you are asked to do something you cannot do, then be honest. Hopefully, he or she will understand.

What do you do if you feel that you have very few friends? Do not wait for people to come to you or extend themselves to you, become the one who does the extending. Join a group of people you can be comfortable with, ask someone out to dinner, or start with lunch. Build a cadre of professional friends. Have a dinner party or go to the movies. Start somewhere.

Sometimes friendship is hard work. Sometimes you expect more of your friends than is reasonable. Sometimes you do not communicate fully. Sometimes you just have a bad day. Being sensitive to all of these pressures will enable you to be the kind of friend you want to find in others.

What does this have to do with karma? For those on a spiritual path, the path of friendship is very important. This is the path of spiritual experience, practicing what you preach; being the person you talk about being and living that truth every day. Friendship is a test of spiritual truth. Are you practicing what you have learned, even if it is really difficult? Perhaps your answer is that you are a work in progress. You can begin to love, forgive, enjoy and cherish the people you are finding in your life. If you find yourself becoming more and more patient and compassionate, than you are really beginning to live that life of living and teaching only love and friendship.

## The Karmic Opportunity

Friendship is the opportunity to open up your heart to others.

Friendship is frequently inconvenient and hence is precisely the power of the karmic opportunity.

Friendship is the opportunity for service at times of crisis in the other person's life.

Friendship is the opportunity to celebrate the success of others with a genuine heart.

Friendship invites you to love without judgment.

Friendship encourages you to trust.

## Prayer

Heavenly Father, please assist me in becoming your tool for service in all of my friendships. Please help me to bring light to all of my relationships and guide me in the best, most helpful and karmically correct words to say to all those I treasure in my life. Amen.

Everyday Karma

## Week 30  Doing a Good Job

So many people hate their jobs. Think about conversations with friends and family members. So many people are profoundly unhappy with what they do every day because of their work environment, their bosses, or the ethical compromises they have to routinely make. Despite this, the jobs that each of us hold are important, and significant to someone.

For example, while in Virginia Beach helping my sister and her family, we decided to rent a movie at the video store. We knew the actors of the film, but could not come up with the name. One of the employees asked if he could help. He was cheerful and genuinely seemed to want to help. We gave him the name of the actors and the gist of the film and he said: "Oh, that's The Legend of Bagger Vance - why we have it right here." He handed us the video and asked if we needed anything else and then he discretely stepped away.

This is a terrific film that seems to be mostly about golf, but the truth is that it's focus is so much more. This film is about grief, healing, and about regaining your balance so that you can "find your swing," your way back to clarity. This is an excellent film for anyone who is grieving, and we certainly needed this gentle film that night. The employee did not know our situation - that we had just lost a child. He did his job in that moment to the best of his ability. He really helped us. We really appreciated him. Indirectly he contributed to our healing process, without knowing it.

We need every person to do their job to the best of their ability in every moment - not just airline pilots, train conductors, physicians, police men and women but even the seemingly insignificant jobs where we are not quite sure that what we are doing really matters. The energy we put into everything matters, it defines our integrity and it defines our karmic path. No energy is ever wasted.

If you hate your job or some aspect of it, try focusing instead on the benefit you are doing for someone each day. You may still dislike aspects of your task or environment, but you will give your very best to the people who matter the most: the public, the customer in front of you, your family and, finally, yourself. You will then find that at least some part of your day will be positive because you are using this as an opportunity to make a difference.

## The Karmic Opportunity

Every day is an opportunity to make a difference in the life of someone.

Every moment we live matters in some aspect.

Learning that we matter enables us to have faith in ourselves, to find meaning in the mundane trivia of the ordinariness of our lives.

Reminding ourselves that what we do matters, restores our critical sense of self-esteem.

Believe in yourself every single day!

## Affirmation

What I do matters to someone every single day, no matter how challenging my days may be.

The Lightworker's Guide to

## Week 31  Psychic Addictions

There was a fascinating article in the San Diego Union-Tribune of March 9th, 2006 about people who are addicted to using the services of psychics, spending up to $1000 a month on phone psychics and/or psychic readers. While the article noted that Gallup polls indicate that most of the population does have some belief in the paranormal, there are always a few who take that belief into an obsession.

What is a psychic addiction? Like anything else, this type of addiction can vary by degrees from the pretty harmless to the completely obsessed. Many people read their horoscopes in the daily newspaper, or their monthly horoscopes in the back of women's magazines. Some people read their horoscopes on-line. The next level is having your horoscope done for you on a personal/professional basis. Some people study the stars so consistently that their entire lives are ruled by the interpretations of star charts - and virtually every astrologer will give you a slightly different interpretation. Some people do not make a move unless they have consulted their charts.

The next level of addiction regards those who consult different types of psychics for readings on their future. These psychics can range anywhere from the neon signed palm readers, to the online psychics who charge exorbitant amounts of money per minute. Either way, these people tap into someone's need to find security in knowing the future. There are also individuals who consult their own fortune telling cards on a consistent basis. These cards of divination can be all levels of Tarot cards, to Runes, or to the seemingly lightest Angel cards. No matter what label you place on them, if you are using them to get answers - you are using them for fortune telling.

Some people consult a psychic as a whim, perhaps with friends, maybe once in their life. Other people go to the extreme and consult psychics every day, allowing the psychic to have tremendous power over them. The person thinks they are getting a leg up on the future, but what they do not realize is that they are giving all their power away to another person who uses their power and energy for themselves. That energy is the money that is paid and the energetic fear that is created. This fear is the trepidation of making a move without knowing what the future holds and the false belief that anyone can consistently tell you what that future holds. No one can do that.

One interesting aspect of fortune telling is the conscious or unconscious manipulation of the future by the psychic. This type of psychic tells you just enough to entice you to return to learn a bit more and a bit more. With each 'reading' you learn enough to be either elated or afraid. The psychic encourages you to share all that is happening in your life. As you begin to share, you may find that some of the insignificant things that the psychic predicts may be coming true. This is because the psychic 'creates a reality' of what can happen. This sets the stage for a probable reality in the mind of the seeker. Eventually the seeker so wants to believe that what the psychic says is true, that sometimes he or she creates the very reality the psychic predicts. In a sense, the seeker relinquishes a certain portion of his or her own free will to the psychic to be able to continually return.

How can it be that a psychic will seem to know something about a person even if that person has told them very little? Perhaps some fortunetellers are just good at listening to your story. Some cleverly figure out that you always go for 'bad boys,' have a string of failed relationships or you have a history of trouble with money and predicting that that behavior will continue does not require a crystal ball. Even if you have your future told only once, the odds are that, even 50 years later, you will remember quite clearly whatever the fortuneteller told you. Why is this? Because, like it or not, whatever that fortuneteller tells you will absolutely influence your future. You will wait to see if it comes true or you will unconsciously set yourself up to have it come true. That is a lot of power and energy to give away.

Why would anyone literally give personal power away to someone else? Because people want to know how it will all work out. Many people are fearful of an unknown future, especially if they think it involves loneliness. The irony is that most people want to know about love. Will she find Mr. Right or will he find the girl of his dreams? Will anyone become beautiful and loveable by consulting a fortuneteller? No one ever does. The real work with spiritual practitioners is very hard work because you have to come face to face with yourself. Then you can consciously choose to change and as you change, everyone around you responds to your new positive life. Fortunetellers do not want you to change. They need you to stay in your emotional and spiritual 'rut.'

You have an infinite number of futures. Each moment is predicated on the decisions you have made in the previous moment. Also, you are affected by what other people do. It has been said that life is frequently what happens while you are making other plans. The whole point of life is that you learn from your experiences and you apply this knowledge, this hard-won wisdom to your unfolding future.

You never ever really need anyone to tell you your future, even for fun. The more sophisticated you become spiritually, the more you are able to connect to the higher planes for the acquisition of wisdom through experience and thoughtful choices. Perhaps the biggest lesson here is the aspect of owning your own life. When you go to anyone else to tell your future, you give part of that ownership away. It is better not to give your power away. It is always preferably to be the captain of your own ship as you guide yourself through the seas of your life.

There are people who are clairvoyant and can see bits and pieces of the future. The honest ones will tell you that theirs is a challenging life and most of them will not routinely tell fortunes.

Asking for help to guide you to your highest good through prayer and positive spiritual connection will enable you to maintain ownership of your life and will, in the end, offer you a much more positive future.

# The Karmic Opportunity

Own your own life. Don't give your power away to fortunetellers and psychics who want to take your energy.

Love the life you are living in all its varied experiences.

Believe in yourself – you absolutely have what it takes to have a wonderful life.

The future is yours to create. Break any psychic addictions and choose to live a much happier life.

## Affirmations

I control my future and my future is wonderful!

My good works, great ideas and wonderful life create my future every day and in every way.

## Week 32   The Nature of Forgiveness

### Understanding Our Perceptions
Why is forgiveness so hard?

Perhaps forgiveness is challenging because there is always a part of you that believes that to forgive someone for something that happened means what that person did to you is okay. You may feel that forgiveness absolves the wrong doer of responsibility.

Some people believe that:

... by forgiving a past hurt, it means that either it was not that serious in the first place or you were overly emotional about it and that it did not warrant the emotion that you gave it at the time.

... by forgiving a person for a terrible transgression, you do not believe that they need to be punished for the pain that they caused.

... you have to wait for the other person to say that they are sorry before you can forgive them.

... you can just say "I forgive you" and all is better now, even if the other person is not sorry and the words you are saying do not really mean anything.

...if the person died and you did not forgive them while they were living, then you cannot ever forgive them for what happened.

...their religious dogma requires forgiveness to get into heaven. These people believe that if they do not forgive someone for something then they are the bad person. It does not particularly matter what the situation is, they are just required to forgive.

Oftentimes family members do abhorrent things to each other. Tragically, parents do horrific things to their children. Eventually, these same children are just expected to forgive this parent and the life-altering, personality-changing action, as if it did not really happen.

The nature of forgiveness is one of the lessons you spend many lifetimes learning. Why does this particular lesson take so long? It takes a long time because it is not a simple lesson; it is complicated. There is theme and variation in all of life and this includes the concepts of what forgiveness means. It very often means very different things to different people.

There was once a television commentator who urged a man who was falsely accused of raping a woman to forgive her for sending him to prison for seven years, to forgive her on national television, to forgive her as she sat in front of him. The accuser's apology was half-hearted. The commentator kept urging the man to just forgive his accuser. Perhaps this famous commentator wanted to raise her ratings. Whatever her reason, she did not understand anything about the nature of forgiveness. The awkwardness on screen was the real story. He was not ready to say those words and the shame the commentator tried to create in him did not make him deny himself.

This is an important point. Forgiveness takes time. Real forgiveness is tremendous and if it does not live within you, then it is not real.

Whatever the experience to be forgiven is, it happened for a reason. Part of the lesson is forgiveness, but it cannot be felt until the person understands the experience in the first place, why it happened and how to apply the lesson of this experience to the rest of his or her life.

Forgiveness is literally a sorting out process for all of life's poignantly painful experiences. Perhaps forgiveness is the byproduct of the acquisition of wisdom.

When a sincere person sorts through a powerful hurt and he or she realizes the lesson, what begins to awaken in them is an understanding that he or she is not afraid of that hurtful or terrifying person any more. That hurtful person can no longer hurt them. Once the fear is removed, he or she can begin to distance themselves from the event or series of events.

Forgiveness is not done for the benefit of the perpetrator: it is done primarily for the benefit of the victim. Whatever an evil person has done, this action earns that person negative karmic points. When you forgive that person, your forgiveness does not necessarily change the karma created by that original evil action. Forgiving the person begins to liberate you, enhancing your karmic path. This only happens if the forgiveness is sincere, because you stop being in resonance with the awful event and you begin to rise above it. That shift in resonance occurs only in tiny increments. Forgiveness itself usually occurs in tiny increments as well. However, this is not as important as the concept that you are moving forward with your life. That terrifying persecutor is no longer exercising power over you. You are taking your power back whether it is from a parent, teacher, friend or stranger.

# The Lightworker's Guide to

Many faiths encourage you to 'just forgive the person or the situation' and you will feel better. Most truly honest people will notice that when they try to do that, they do not necessarily feel any better. They cannot feel better, because the truth is that the feeling of release, which comes from genuine forgiveness, is not there.

Sometimes a person will say that they have already forgiven a person for a terrible wrong but they still feel a tremendous rage toward that person. Their mouth is moving, but the forgiveness is not there. They can say it a thousand times, but if it does not live within them, it is not true.

## The Process of Forgiveness

When someone has hurt you or someone you love, you may find that you are tremendously angry. You have to work through that anger. Talking about it is critically important. You cannot just 'get over it.' You have to discuss it, look at various points of view, and talk about how you feel about the ramifications of the event and how you are changed. If trauma occurred, you have to acknowledge that as well and begin to get to the other side of the trauma to begin to trust again. Sometimes the event makes you extremely angry, creating a level of outrage. This can be its own trauma - how could something like this happen?

Working through outrage and trauma are going to take time. It could last one month, three years, ten years or even much longer. The length of time for getting past outrage and into a healing/accepting mode is in direct proportion to the level of the outrage. All things are a function of degree.

The process of getting through this is the Schoolhouse of Earthly Experience. So, first you just have to live through the moments of the drama of it all. Then as you get past the initial trauma/drama, you begin to look for answers. Then you look for blame. Blame is always a critical issue in healing. Obviously someone is responsible for this and they have to be brought to justice. There is a feeling sometimes that you cannot heal until you can be sure that this can never happen again to someone else. The 'who is responsible' process is quite time consuming and often utterly essential to any formal healing, much less forgiveness. It takes time to understand all that has happened. And then sometimes there is no one to blame when something life changing and horrific happens.

However, what if you are to blame? What if you caused the trauma because of something you did or did not do? What if you have to forgive yourself? What if you have decided that you can never forgive yourself? How many future lives will you punish yourself? When is it okay to forgive yourself?

You live in a world of nanoseconds and nanotechnology. You live in the world of the super fast reaction, response and action. However, when going through any type of trauma, nothing happens quickly after the event. Everything seems to take forever and that includes the 'getting-over-it-part.'

Let's say that you are past the initial trauma, and that you have gone beyond the seemingly endless waves of grief. You are functioning in life again. You can get through a day without bringing it up or crying. You seem just fine on the outside. People around you breathe a sigh of relief, thinking that their friend or family member is going to be OK again. They will return to who they used to be with you, and your relationship will go back to 'normal.'

However, 'normal' is now completely relative. The person you were is gone forever. The person you are becoming is still evolving; you are still healing. You force yourself to do the ordinary things. At some point someone brings up the forgiveness issue and you cringe. How can this be forgiven? If it was deliberate, forgiveness is often unthinkable. If it is you who need to be forgiven, this may not be something you can even discuss. But it has to be thinkable. God always forgives you. God always finds a way to help a situation to heal. All can be forgiven in some way and in some fashion. You just have to find that way or fashion. This powerful exercise can help.

List the event.

Then list at least one powerful emotion that is still operable because of this event.

Finally, list what lesson you learned from this event.

For example, if your father died when you were six, then his death is the event. Now list the main emotion you felt at his death. Finally begin to list what that event and its emotion have taught you. What was the lesson learned? The point of the difficulty is the lesson. If you do not get the lesson, karma will have to repeat it for you. Not a happy thought! So, the main focus is: what did you learn? In the example of the death, you learned what it felt like to be without that parent.

Perhaps abandonment was the emotion. So you would have learned compassion for all children who lose a parent. You would have understood that fear is a subtle part of your everyday life without that dad there to protect you. You would have watched as your mother had to take over both roles and struggle and you would have learned how you had to help her and take on different roles yourself. Think of the lessons that this particular death would have provided. Every death has a purpose, and every experience is designed to teach you something.

You may have to do this same exercise over and over. Write each event down so that you can really put your feelings in black and white. Eventually, you will desensitize yourself from these events entirely. When someone asks you about any of these powerful life-changing events, you will be able to relate each one with less and less emotion. Understanding the lessons will also give you a leg up on the forgiveness process.

As you grow spiritually, you begin to look for the more subtle elements of the lessons to be learned from any event. Every event has an echo factor, like dropping a pebble in a pool, the energy of the event just keeps going out. There does come a critical juncture where you have to decide you are going to heal. The lessons of the event - as horrible or traumatic as they are - are profoundly valuable.

The Tibetans say that your enemy is your greatest teacher. The reason why you have terrible things happen in your life is to learn from them. As you constantly open yourself up to learning from this powerful experience, you begin to grow. You stop surviving each day and begin to live each day. You look for the reason the event to be forgiven, happened. The more you live and love, the more the concept of forgiveness becomes a real possibility and this process just takes time.

Always remember that just because someone does not talk about their experience, does not mean that they are 'over it.' Most people spend a lifetime working through traumas on very subtle levels.

## Forgiveness in Healing 'What If?' Scenarios

What if the same terrible crime that caused you to grieve in a powerful way was committed life after life and you responded the same way over and over? What if in this life, you learned from the event and forgave the aspect of it that connected you to the event? Would you heal the karmic burden? Could this possibly stop the event from being repeated in the next life?

What if the death of a beloved partner kept happening life after life so that you could finally learn to forgive him or her for leaving and learn to live a whole life with a new person? Was the lesson here healing grief or letting go of attachment – or both?

What if someone you thought you loved, really loved someone else and you were angry at that person life after life? What if you stopped being angry with them, and thanked them for giving you a different experience? What if you have a tremendous life with a different love? Can you now forgive the previous person you thought you were meant for, and begin to love life completely differently? Was the lesson here a release from attachment and the opportunity to forgive and live a happier life?

What if you were distracted and left your baby in a hot car and your precious child died? How do you ever forgive yourself for that lapse in memory? How can anyone else forgive you? What if you see yourself as totally unforgivable and forever unlovable? You must always remember that God will forgive you. You must find a way to atone for the event, and the path of atonement will allow you to eventually forgive yourself. At some point, you have to want to be forgiven; you have to want to stop punishing yourself. When you are ready, a door will open and that path to forgiveness, to personal redemption will finally appear.

What if each parent thought the other was watching a child in a pool and that child drowns? Is the purpose of this death solely to teach each parent to stop judging the other and themselves and to learn to forgive?

If someone murders your family can you ever forgive the murderer? Is any murder forgivable? Is such a thing possible? Yes, it is, for as long as the hate lives within you, you will be in resonance with the murder drama. When you rise above hate on that level, you can set yourself free. And in an ironic way, you also set the murder victims free.

## Forgiveness in Many Forms

In the movie Shawshank Redemption, the main character is falsely accused, wrongly convicted and given life in prison for murdering his wife. The story is one of learning a life lesson. In his case, he realized that he had repeatedly failed his wife as a husband. Once the lesson was learned, he was able to escape that prison: that physical, mental, emotional and spiritual prison he had lived in for so long. He also took with him the lessons of the entire experience.

What if you have a terrible parent who is vicious, and sexually abusive, and has made your life hell? Let us say that that parent dies when you are in your twenties. You spit on this parent's grave at the funeral. You vow never to forgive this terrible person. Let us say that you mature and find yourself in your fifties or sixties and want to heal your life. Is it too late to find a path to forgiving this terrible parent? Of course it is not too late. Time only has a meaning on the Earth plane; it does not exist where the parent is now. The opportunity to find meaning in the terrible suffering is without time limit. Learning about the situation and allowing yourself to heal, allowing yourself to find your own power, and your strength of character, will take you down that path of forgiveness and eventually spiritual growth.

No matter, which 'what if' you look at, and no matter how you look at it, there is always a path to the place where you can forgive all the players in any given situation. You can even forgive yourself.

Perhaps one of the most powerful situations you can study is the one from the Nazi concentration camps. How did these astounding people who survived the unspeakable acts of the Nazis learn to live again and learn to forgive? How was this ever possible? How do you forgive an individual or a group of individuals for massacring not just your family, but also your heritage? How do you forgive a group of people who sought to destroy your very soul?

The answer to this question bears careful consideration. It is very important to study the frame of reference of the many Jewish souls who survived the extermination camps. You must also study the extermination of the Tibetans and their entire way of life by the Chinese communists. No culture has a corner on the suffering market and these are but two powerful examples of enlightened souls who have chosen to live a life of forgiveness.

Many Jewish survivors went on to become thriving businesspeople, and to rebuild their families. Many of them never accepted the label of survivor/victim. Many of them were fierce in their desire to live all the way, to live so well and so strongly that they would insist that the world learn the lessons that the Nazis taught and that were so hard won. Many Jewish witnesses to the Nazi horror forgave the Nazis because once they forgave them, they got their power back. Only these stalwart witnesses could choose to forgive and embrace this terrifying experience. The world owes them a debt of gratitude for doing all they have done to remind us of the worst and the best of humanity and how it took place.

The Tibetan example is just as chilling and horrible. Monasteries and ecosystems were utterly destroyed and their entire way of life was desecrated. The Tibetans do not hate the Chinese and, in fact, have forgiven them. They have not denied the Chinese their evil experience, nor have they been silent, but have offered the world the view that goodness does prevail and they have used this opportunity to show the world the face of forgiveness, of what it means to really live your truth.

No one has a monopoly on suffering. Everyone suffers in some way. However, the souls that advance through soul evolution learn how to forgive what created the suffering experience and use it to create a life of thriving experience. Ultimately, it is the path to forgiveness that sets all of you free and allows a modest promotion on the path of soul evolution. Remember, forgiveness takes time: there is no timetable for completing the forgiveness process.

## The Karmic Opportunity
### Understanding Our Perceptions

Forgiveness heals the forgiving person.

Forgiving someone does not absolve him or her of wrongdoing.

Karma always balances all actions.

The karma created by the hurt caused will be returned to the hurtful person in some way and in some time because this is how the Universe works.

Karma is always fair and balanced.

You can forgive someone no matter how long ago the person died.

Blind, emotionless forgiveness is worthless.

If genuine forgiveness does not live within you, then it is not real.

Forgiveness takes time, often years to acquire.

When you learn the lesson of the experience, you can release fear.

When you are no longer afraid of the perpetrator, you begin to set yourself free.

When you have set yourself free, you begin to acquire wisdom.

When you acquire wisdom, you can create within yourself a feeling of release and newfound freedom.

### The Process of Forgiveness

Before forgiveness can take place, you have to process the emotion attached to the event.

If you are responsible for a terrible situation, then you have to process the emotion, learn the lessons and decide that you can be forgiven. Be patient with yourself.

Learning from the traumatic experience means that you have to identify each event, each emotion, and each lesson learned.

### Forgiveness in Healing 'What If?' Scenarios

You can heal your life after a terrible trauma through the process of forgiveness.

Study the examples of how other people have learned from their traumas and have healed.

Everyone is grieving or has grieved something. Happy are they who have healed their grief and embraced the lessons of the experience.

Everyone's process of forgiveness is unique.

There is never a timetable for forgiving a person or a situation.

## Prayer

Heavenly Father, please grant me the wisdom to learn from even the most tragic experience. Please help me to have the patience to work through the emotions and to embrace loving life and the people in it, again. Help me to heal my wounded heart and to know your love and forgiveness now and forever. Amen.

The Lightworker's Guide to

## Week 33   The Brother of the Penitent Man

In the Old Testament of the Bible, there is the story of the man with two sons. One son is the good son, always doing the right thing, generous, caring, and standing by his parents and his family. The other son is the black sheep, doing bad things and he does not stand by his parents and family. It is this son who leaves home.

The black sheep son goes on a long journey of fully tasting the experiences of the dark side of life. His family is ashamed to say that he is their son and they despair that he will ever find a way out of that darkness. They pray for him. They pray that he will eventually find the strength and courage to overcome his karmic weaknesses and find his way back to God and, hopefully, to his family.

In the meantime, the good son stands by his parents, marries, raises his own family, and is a fine upstanding citizen. Everyone loves him. He is sure his parents, especially his father, are very proud of him. He works hard to do such a good job with his life and be the son his black sheep brother is not. He tries to make up to his father for what his brother does not seem to ever be able to be: a good person.

Now sometimes in life, a miracle occurs. In this case, the black sheep son discovers the error of his ways and decides to clean up his act. He stops doing terrible things. He can see the pain that he has caused and he now lives in anguish at the harm that he has brought to others, especially his family. He is not sure they can ever forgive him but he decides to try and, eventually, returns home. He is penitent and decides to ask his family, especially his father, for forgiveness. He tells them in advance that he is coming.

His father is so thrilled that his black sheep son has seen the light, and the error of his previous ways, that he makes plans for a great party to welcome this transformed son home. He showers this son with attention. This father sheds tears of gratitude that his son has returned to him. The ever-good son now has to decide how he feels about all of this. Perhaps, he has two choices in how he can approach this situation. Ultimately, this is an opportunity for the good son to descend to a lower spiritual level, or rise, to a higher spiritual level.

In option one, the good son can choose to look at this from the point of view of jealousy: he has been the good son, stood by his parents and worked all his life to make up to his father for what this other brother is not. When the father makes such a big fuss over the changes in his formerly black sheep son, the good son can feel a burning sense of betrayal that his father has not honored him for his own good deeds and loyalty. Where is his party? Resentment may become the ultimate result in which case he may find himself descending into a new kind of darkness of jealousy and an emotion bordering on hate. He does not realize that his emotions may be based on a fear of the loss of his father's love and attention. He no longer has the foil of his black sheep brother's bad deeds upon which to reflect his bright light. Now the father has two wonderful sons. The good son now thinks he has to establish a new identity and this is a spiritual challenge for him.

The other choice the good son has is the path of spiritual wisdom. The wise person will know that perhaps we have all walked that path of darkness and found our way home. That path home is a very challenging pathway and sometimes it is torturous. We have all felt the guilt of shame at our previous behavior. We have asked for forgiveness and hoped that this could be available to us. We all hope to be welcomed home by our fathers: our mortal parent and our spiritual parent, our Father who is in heaven. Neither the mortal parent nor God loves either son less. Both parental figures love both sons for the path each has taken. However, it is a rite of passage to be 'welcomed home' both on Earth and in heaven when any soul emerges from darkness.

The wise brother will also welcome the penitent brother home because he has prayed for his brother's healing. His prayers and the prayers of his family have, in fact, been answered. In the aspect of the generosity of his own welcoming heart, he acquires the wisdom of God. We are brothers, fathers, sons, and friends. The growth of one person is the growth of us all. Perhaps the test of the black sheep is not for him alone but for all of us to hold dear the hope that we can all be welcomed home and forgiven for our sins.

The strength of one strengthens us all. This wise brother will know deep inside of himself that perhaps, in another lifetime, he was that black sheep and his father welcomed him home. He may also know that his own fondest wish was that his past life good brother would also welcome him and honor him with his love.

In this current situation, this wise brother would know at the core level, that his father could not love him less and that his black sheep brother's transformation will bring joy to the entire family because their grief and aching hearts can now be healed. As each person heals, so are we all healed.

So, in the end, the wise brother can acquire great spiritual benefit by the enlightenment of a black sheep brother. The wise brother will also avoid the pitfall of jealousy, the fear that there is not enough for him. Fearlessness is one of the many signs of a wise person.

As the good brother generously welcomes the awakening of the formerly black sheep brother, he may find a new delight in the friendship and companionship of this brother. Patience, prayer, goodness and generosity are always their own rewards.

## The Karmic Opportunity

Jealousy is fear with a grasping face. Recognize that there is always great abundance in the world for all of us.

Wisdom is the ability to see the value in the experience in any situation without judgment.

The wise person is always generous with his or her love and aware that the spiritual path is the path of the lessons of learning to love others as ourselves, and often that path involves tolerance and forgiveness of others.

We always have a choice in how we will approach any situation and every choice carries with it a powerful karmic opportunity and result.

## Prayer

Dear Lord, please help me to make wise choices. Help me to hear the wisest path to living a loving life. Thank you for the powerful experiences I have had which enable me to grow spiritually. Amen.

## Week 34   Karmic Challenges

What is a karmic challenge? A karmic challenge can be many things. We are presented with many challenges in our lives but some of them are far more significant than others. Each decision we make becomes a logic trail and sets us up for the next event.

However, every so often, we are placed in a position where we must make a very significant karmic decision -- one that can elevate us from where we are currently standing emotionally to a much higher level. These karmic challenges can be anything from healing after the death of a child, a divorce or job loss. A challenge can be facing the hurt of childhood abuse. It can be healing a past life when awareness is presented of this past life. It can also be forgiving and learning from an event that deeply hurt us. This karmic moment requires several important criteria to be present:

We recognize the moment and acknowledge hearing our Higher Selves speaking in our ears.

We acknowledge that the karmic moment exists and that we have to do something about it.

We have the courage to think about responding.

We respond by taking advantage of the opportunity.

We continue to take advantage -- for the foreseeable future -- of this karmic challenge.

We build on this karmic challenge in preparation for the next significant one to come, and they come far more frequently once we take advantage of the first one.

## Let us analyze how people respond to these karmic challenges:

Some people see an opportunity in front of them, recognize it, and decide that they just cannot deal with it.

Some people see it, begin to take advantage of it, get scared that their lives might change and stop doing anything further.

Some people take advantage of it just long enough to see what can change and then consciously choose not to go any further.

Some people take that opportunity all the way to a significantly wonderful outcome. What kind of opportunities/challenges might these be?

## Let us study these examples:

A teacher appears to help us out of the spiritual darkness and we take advantage of the opportunity to grow on every spiritual level. We find that we are changed forever.

We get to become a teacher for someone else. This is a wonderful opportunity to be of tremendous service. Helping another person find his or her true spiritual self is helping them to know his or her own wonderful level of goodness.

We take a job that we did not think we could do and it changes us. Our courage carries us through those moments of self-doubt and our confidence grows. We use this karmic challenge to rise to the occasion of our own growth.

We have an adventure that helps us to learn about who we really are. There are those types of adventures that significantly test all of the elements of courage within us. Adventures are karmic opportunities to see the depth of our inner strength.

We perform a great service for someone. This could be something profound such as helping a loved one as they go through the final moments of their dying process. Our kind words help him or her to release attachment to earthly life. We can also help a grieving relative release attachment to a person who has died. The service can also be as seemingly minor as being a good teacher for a child. The ramifications of honestly teaching someone to follow a positive path are beyond calculation.

We find ourselves in a position to show great courage and we do so. Every moment of great courage is a karmic challenge to conquer fear and to really know who we are. This courageous moment could be that we are in mortal danger, we are in a terrible accident and have to heal or we have to face the loss of someone precious to us.

We find ourselves in a position to be very jealous of someone else's good fortune. Maybe she had a baby and we cannot. Maybe he got the promotion we desperately wanted. Perhaps she got to have the wedding, spouse, or house we had always dreamed of having. This karmic moment offers us the option of sending jealously packing and recognizing that there is always plenty in the universe and that jealousy, that pesky fear with a grasping face, need not be part of who we are.

The happier we are for that fortunate person in front of us, the more we can profoundly grow spiritually.

Whatever the moment, every karmic challenge that is presented empowers us to face our fear, to be different; to make a difference, and to know that we are going to be just fine no matter what happens. Sometimes this opportunity makes us feel significantly better about ourselves because it takes us farther along our spiritual path and, ultimately, we are happier.

We may also review our life and note those times of karmic challenge where we did well. This type of review will also show us how we could have done things differently if we are not happy with a particular outcome. Ultimately, every karmic challenge is, in the end, a life experience. We must always be mindful to stay out of a place of judgment for how things turned out for us, whether they were good or not so good. Perhaps that is the ultimate karmic challenge: ceasing judgment of all that happens and simply standing as the observer to the progress of life.

## The Karmic Opportunity

Seek to recognize the karmic moment, by remembering to hear your Higher Self.

Acknowledge that the karmic moment exists and that you have to do something about it.

Have the courage to think about responding.

Respond by taking advantage of the opportunity.

Continue to take advantage -- for the foreseeable future -- of this karmic challenge.

Build on this karmic challenge in preparation for the next significant one to come, and they come far more frequently once you take advantage of the first one.

## Affirmations

I am comfortable recognizing the karmic opportunity when it arises.

I have the courage to seek the wisdom to take the karmically correct action.

The Lightworker's Guide to

# Week 35   The Difference Between Enabling vs Empowering

## Enabling

What is the difference between the concepts of enabling a person and empowering a person? Sometimes that line seems somewhat confusing. First, we will discuss the concepts of enabling. Then, we will contrast this with empowering a person and the dynamic results this can produce.

To enable a person in the psychological sense is to pretty much keep them where they are so that they can continue to do or be what they have always been. We enable someone to continue to survive, but they do not really grow, they just continue to sort of drift through life.

The best examples of this are parents who give their kids whatever they want. They never teach their children how life works. They never challenge the child to be a stronger person, to learn discipline, or to learn to achieve successful goals. They are so afraid the child will not love them if they enforce rules, discipline or dare to say no to the child that they give in to the child's every demand. These parents enable their children to misbehave, or do harm to themselves or to eventually, be unable to function in society. Even then, that same parent lets their child live at home, gives them money and supports them so that the child never really matures into a contributing adult. They enable them to drift from day to day. Their emotional and intellectual engines stay forever in idle, stagnant in existence. Maybe that parent was enabled him or herself, and simply does not know how to be a real parent. This is not a criticism of parents, but an observation that generations of enabling behavior continue to roll on with little change.

Some families abuse their children, enabling them to barely survive without ever teaching them how to grow or showing them what success and self esteem look and feel like. This is also true for families of drug or alcohol dependent family members where they look the other way and just let the family member keep getting away with the destructive behavior. They pretend that it is OK for that parent or sibling to continue to drink, gamble or use drugs because they themselves feel powerless to stop them. By the time this situation is dangerously critical, there is precious little that a family member can do other than not supply the destructive things.

Sometimes, the person has to decide for him or herself to finally grow. This then becomes the life experience: he or she can now choose to heal his or her destructive past and work toward a brighter future.

Some families enable an abuser to continue to cause harm through spiritual, physical or incest abuse. This parent becomes a grandparent and great grandparent and just continues perpetrating this same despicable behavior. When one family member says no or tries to stop the abuse, he or she becomes the outcast.

It takes real courage to stand up to enabling behavior. Sometimes a person has to get help to do it.

Often, a boss, minister, teacher or even a physician can be extremely abusive. However, just because that person appears to be an authority figure does not mean that you can look the other way and hope that it will somehow get better.

People keep receiving abuse because everyone enables the abuser to continue this behavior. The act of omission, knowing it is going on and looking the other way, creates its own karmic return. Eventually, the victim seeks people who will continue to enable them to be abused because that behavior is all they know. Then, tragically, they abuse their children and the cycle continues. It does not always have to be this way: life can change.

## Empowering

Empowerment is teaching a person how to grow, how to grow in a tremendous way, and to provide tools for this growth. This process helps the individual to recognize the power he or she can possess within him or herself. Teaching someone that they possess power for things so wonderful, so positive that they are changed forever and everyone they touch is also better for the encounter, is a dynamic prospect.

Empowerment is the core element in teaching. Give a person food and he eats for a day. Give a person seeds to plant and teach him how to grow things, and you empower that person to eat forever.

Empowerment is the basis for teaching self-esteem. Self-esteem is the one thing that no amount of money can buy; it has to be earned. Giving is not always better than receiving if the giving is done to emotionally cripple or control a person. Eventually, that which is given is no longer appreciated and comes to hold no value whatsoever. Slowly and insidiously, the controller begins to see their control slip from their fingers.

Empowerment is the sole basis for independence. The job of every parent and teacher is to create ever-increasing levels of independence in their children and students. As you teach people to do something, hold them accountable for the results and then praise them for their accomplishments. In this way, you are creating successful building blocks. These building blocks are the very foundation for the construction of a pathway the person creates to go to the next level. These success blocks can also establish the foundation for greater and greater levels of achievement and, ultimately, responsibility. Literally, the person is creating his or her own dynamic future of positive independent living.

An excellent example is learning to cook. All human beings eat and all human beings need to know how to cook at least some things so that they can be independent and care for themselves. Unfortunately, many parents do not teach their children to cook. (The reasons for this can be that the parent does not know how or they feel that the child is not interested.) Teaching a child to cook can be messy and costly. It takes great patience to teach someone to cook. You have to deal with dangerous things like stoves, ovens, knives and electricity, all of which can cause harm or actually be destructive. You have to teach sanitation so that infected or bad food is not used. There is quite a bit to learn. However, teaching someone to cook is one of the most rewarding things for a parent/teacher to do. Here are the requirements:

- Patience - you will have to explain things over and over. Patience is the key to the growth process.
- Diligence - you will have to continually teach a variety of aspects, with every meal.
- Energy - it takes lots of energy to oversee a task without interfering too much. The student has to experience the process all the way.
- Emotional stability - you have to be secure enough in yourself to teach something to someone else. There is always the possibility that your student will exceed you. You have to be okay with that, you have to actually enjoy where your student can take the knowledge you are sharing.
- Humility - you have to step aside when the student wants to do things for him or herself, to show you what he or she has learned.
- Responsibility – hold the student accountable for all actions. He or she must take responsibility for what did not work as well as what did work.
- Mindfulness - you have to pay meticulous attention to what you say. Criticism will completely destroy what you are trying to teach. Every single error is a critical element in learning. Sometimes learning what does not work is more valuable than learning what does work. Never criticize errors. Ask your student what was learned. There is value in what appear to be mistakes.

Whatever you teach, from physics to mechanics, fashion design to spelling, be sure to give the person in front of you your very best.

Empowerment is giving of yourself for the betterment of others, giving them a boost up, and sharing your knowledge. Mindfulness is the essence of empowerment, one of the key elements of living a life based on the generosity of love.

## The Karmic Opportunity

Enabling cripples people and can lead them down a sad and dark path.

Enabling is a spineless action, geared to either weakness or its handmaiden, powerful control.

Empowerment is holding the person in front of you accountable with wisdom and guidance.

Empowerment is helping people find their independence, their courage and physical, mental, emotional and spiritual growth.

Empowerment is giving of yourself for the betterment of others, giving them a boost up, and sharing your knowledge.

Mindfulness is the essence of empowerment, one of the key elements of living a life based in the generosity of love.

## Prayer

Dear Lord, I pray for the knowledge to be a wise guide to those who seek my assistance. I pray for wisdom as a parent, friend, co-worker, spouse and family member. Let all of my words be wise and brief and let all of my actions be for the greater good of all. Amen.

The Lightworker's Guide to

## Week 36   Whatever You Want is OK ...

It is probably safe to say that we have all done it, you know, tried to be agreeable, even when we really did not want to do something. It goes something like this:

Question: Hey, let's go out for dinner, or lunch - where do you want to go?

Answer: I don't know, anywhere you want to go is fine with me.

Question: I feel like Mexican food - is that okay?

Answer: Anything is fine with me.

Question: But I thought you hated Mexican food?

Answer: Oh, well, I don't really care where we go.

Question: But are you sure? We can go wherever you want.

Answer: It doesn't matter, I'm okay with anything.

Question: Well, okay, but is there any place that you would particularly like to go?

Answer: No, anything is okay, you know, whatever you want.

The above scenario literally drives people nuts, both the person proposing the location for the dinner and the person trying to be agreeable. It particularly makes men crazy. They just hate it when women do this. Women also do this to each other and they all hate it, but no one wants to be considered pushy or impolite. The end result is that the answer of "anything is okay" ends up looking wishy-washy, which is not necessarily agreeable.

Both the questioner and the responder are trying to easily get along with each other. Neither wants to be dictatorial or demanding. However, the responder is not helping the situation. In some ways, the person who says: "Anything is fine," is usually not really telling the truth about how he or she truly feels. Few people have no opinion on things. However, a surprisingly large number of people are very uncomfortable saying what they really want to do or how they actually feel.

Many people so want to be liked and want to be accepted that they will sacrifice how they really feel about a given situation to keep the peace. Many people want to make the other person happy, so again, they sacrifice themselves; they sacrifice what they would really like to do.

Some people are passive aggressive and insist that the other person make the choice and then they punish that person for the choice. In that scenario, if you make the choice you can get punished for it and if you do not make the choice, you end up deadlocked. That type of scenario is all about power.

Making a decision -- any decision -- takes a certain amount of courage because someone will hold you accountable for it. How can this situation be handled differently?

If someone asks you, then tell him or her that you love Mexican but hate Thai, or you are game for anything but

Southern cooking, or that you are hungry for a steak, or that you just love Italian. Tell people that you are allergic to shellfish, peanuts, chocolate, and eggs or that you do not eat pork. This process of narrowing down the choices helps a lot in deciding where to go.

If you are a visitor in an area and have no idea what is there, it still does not matter, you are human, you have preferences, likes and dislikes which can be honored. Tell your companion.

The point is to give the questioner as much information as possible so that you have an even, balanced exchange. Participate in the decision. However, if you really do not care, then do not criticize the other person's choice. Along the same lines, if it is a great choice then it is important to tell them so. Positive feedback is always appreciated.

The bottom line in any scenario between two people is communication. Step up to the plate and say what you prefer. If you are caught in the situation as the questioner, ask more pertinent questions if the other person is somewhat new to you, such as:

Do you have any preferences?
Are there any foods you do not like?
Is there anything you cannot eat?

When you do this, you are bringing balance to the exchange, furthering good communication, reducing frustration and hopefully having a great time in the process. If all else fails, then just take turns, each person picking the eating-place, alternating times! Enjoy!

## The Karmic Opportunity

I am clear and decisive in my dealings with others.

I am able to communicate my desires so that others can understand me in a positive and productive manner.

It is acceptable to tell people what I would truly like to have or to do.

## Affirmation

When I make a decision or tell someone how I truly feel, I will be accepted for my position.

The Lightworker's Guide to

## Week 37    Personal Power Presence

Is it true that one rotten apple can spoil the barrel? Can the toxicity of one person create such a toxic environment that an office or family event can be ruined almost immediately for many people? Yes, it is absolutely true.

If you remove that person from that environment, can the environment heal? With help, yes, it can.

It is also true that some people create havoc wherever they go, living on the drama of the disasters they create.

We have all seen situations, particularly family situations, where one person's presence and their specific attitude will create a hostile or at least an uncomfortable environment wherever they go. They are the relatives people dread to invite, but feel an obligation to, even if this relative is abusive.

If several toxic people are involved, they act like a collective black cloud over a situation or event and dark emotions are the result. This is the instance of the schoolyard bully encountering kids who are just playing peacefully. The bully always has his or her cronies around, primarily because his or her power is drawn from the weakness of these less morally courageous kids. This bully strolls up and the result is that everyone feels bad after the bullying has taken place.

A personality like this can infect an entire classroom or an entire business. If the head of any organization is really dark emotionally, then the entire organization will be dark – it always filters down the food chain.

What about the reverse? Is it possible for one person's presence to make such a large difference, that it feels as if the sun came out? Can the presence of one specific individual change how an entire organization looks at a situation? Yes, actually, the presence of one person with a dynamic and powerful goodness can transform a tremendous amount of darkness. Additionally, one person can act like a powerful support pillar in an organization, holding it up in the face of great darkness. The irony is that this particular person may be almost invisible, yet you really need them.

Remember Melanie Wilkes in the movie Gone With The Wind? 'Miss Melly' was the glue that held that entire extended family structure together in the face of war, animosity, tremendous loss and illness. She was even subtly dressed in blue and white in almost every scene – the colors of the Virgin Mary - a quiet reference to her spiritual quality. No, she was not too good to be true. These people do exist. Their seeming boring reliability is a lighthouse in the dark.

Why was she so critical to all those people? She was vitally important because she was wise. She often appeared to be the pawn in the political game of family relationships, but she never acted like a pawn. She held her power close and always used it wisely. She even elegantly knew how to handle the extremely powerful and dynamic personalities of Scarlet and Rhett Butler. She was powerful enough to teach Scarlet that there was goodness and unselfishness within her. Melanie was the real leader but she managed this role behind the scenes.

Real change comes about because someone in a family, an organization, or a group of friends acts as the wise leader. This can be quite obvious or extremely subtle as in the case of Melanie Wilkes. Start to look around you and see if you can identify who in your organization or family fills this role. Who is the wise one everyone seems to go to in your office? Who looks out for the greatest good in any political situation?

Notice the patience, wisdom and restraint with which he or she approaches a situation. Wisdom comes from the processing of challenging experiences, which offer us an opportunity to learn new things. We can take this knowledge and apply it with wisdom to future situations. Many organizations do not have a wise one among them. The tragedy is how many people keep making the same mistake. This is not wisdom; it is a questionable use of everyone's energy.

The point here is to look around and see who is making a difference. Help that person. Learn from them. Soon, you will find that the person who is making this difference is you!

## The Karmic Opportunity

Focus on goodness even when the situation appears very dark.

Be the observer of what is happening around you and seek to be that light in the darkness through the wise use of power.

Always seek the greatest good for all the parties concerned.

Allow people to save face while holding them accountable.

## Affirmation

Love backed with power can heal the world because it has the strength to make a positive difference.

## Week 38   Post Traumatic Stress Disorder (PTSD)

### The Utter Loss of the Feeling of Safety

There was an interesting television show that depicted a bizarre situation where one of the stars was at work and suddenly became involved in a hostage situation. Three people are murdered right in front of him. In the follow-on multi-part episodes, the writers explored what happened to our star after this traumatic event. The character discovers that he is not the same and the world that he knew no longer feels safe. The point of the follow-on episodes is what it takes to find the person his family has known before the terrible event, because the man they currently know is not the same person.

An abstract definition of Post Traumatic Stress Disorder would be, in ordinary terms, something that happens in your world that acts like a terrible shock to you. Even if you expect difficult things such as in a war or police situation, the actual reality of it is that, no matter what you think you are prepared for, nothing prepares you for the feeling that your world is now no longer safe.

Safety is the mental and emotional security that allows you to function every day. Safety is like an invisible bubble that surrounds you. You may bump into difficult experiences, but your safety bubble protects you from responding emotionally to the little things. The happier and secure you are as a person, the thicker is your safety bubble or aura.

Your aura is literally the energy that surrounds you. It routinely extends up to a foot or more around your entire body. The stronger your aura, the healthier you feel. The strength of your aura is also reflected in your own strength of character, your confidence and your basic ability to handle stress.

This invisible safety bubble enables you to handle day-to-day stress. The stronger it is, the healthier you are going to be in the long term. The longer you live inside this safety bubble, this strong auric structure, the stronger you feel. There is a subtle sense of power that begins to live within you, a confidence that defines you. This bubble is physical and emotional. This confidence in safety as you go about your life causes you to believe that you live in a safe world.

The problem occurs when something happens that not just pierces that safety bubble, but utterly shatters it. The fact of the matter is that at some point in your life, you are going to experience a traumatic event, as part of living. Lots and lots of people suffer from PTSD to a greater or a lesser degree, because traumatic events happen all around us. There are a variety of events that can happen that you may not consider PTSD, but they are all post-traumatic stress, to a greater or lesser degree. Some examples of PTSD causing events:

- A bomb or bombs goes off.
- All violent events in war.

# The Lightworker's Guide to

- Automobile accidents.
- Automobile accidents with injuries.
- Automobile accidents where someone you love dies.
- Muggings.
- Home Invasion robberies.
- Kidnappings.
- Shootings.
- Fire in your home or office.
- Discovering that your spouse is having an affair.
- Missing Person situations.
- Sudden loss of job - you had no idea it was coming.
- Natural disaster: fire, flood, hurricane, tornado, tsunami and earthquakes. Natural disasters happen so suddenly that you have little or no time to prepare - whatever happens occurs in a blink of an eye.
- Diagnosis of a terrible life-threatening illness.
- Death by heart attack or aneurysm of a loved one.
- Sudden death of someone you love by any means.
- Being stalked by someone
- Rape of someone you love or yourself.
- Request for a divorce when you did not know your marriage had a problem.
- Parents divorcing and you did not know they had a problem.

The characteristic elements of PTSD are these:

# Everyday Karma

- Whatever happens is absolutely sudden.
- The events may be completely unexpected.
- You have a tremendous rush of adrenalin in the body.
- Often you have a fight or flight scenario.
- You survive a horrific event, but others around you die.
- You could not have anticipated the event.
- You may have seconds to respond.
- You have no response option - whatever it is just happens.
- Even if you train for traumatic events, as do medical professionals, soldiers, Federal Agents or police officers, the reality of it is usually very different than the training for it.

## The Continuing Energy of Catastrophic Events

One of the problems with catastrophic events is that they are not immediately over; they keep going. In an automobile accident, the accident itself may be over, almost instantly. However, getting the victim out of the car may be a nightmare, then getting the person to the hospital may take a long time, or there may be extreme weather. Sometimes the traumatic event doesn't seem to end.

In a war scenario, the soldier may have survived a car bombing one minute and the next second is involved in a firefight. In World Wars I and II, soldiers were called 'shell shocked' when they felt this kind of trauma. In the American Civil War, this syndrome was called 'soldier's heart.'

A person may discover that their spouse is asking for a divorce and then find out that he or she is going to remove the children or has left with the children and/or wiped them out financially. It just does not end.

Whatever the nature of the stress, it is unique for the person experiencing it. Each person is going to handle it very, very differently. However, there are various initial responses to the PTSD causing event:

- Pure shock.
- Gratitude that you survived if that was the scenario.
- Horror at the event.
- Devotion to helping those around you in the initial moment.
- Absolutely freezing in place from fear and not responding at all.
- If there is an injury, numbness to the injury - you continue to carry on using the force of adrenalin in the body.
- The body is flooded with adrenalin.
- The memory of the event is seared in the brain because of the adrenalin.
- An unfamiliar sense of rage permeates your entire body.
- Immediate, often profound grief.
- Guilt that you survived and someone else did not.

Once the initial event or events are over, what is going on in the physical, emotional, mental and spiritual body of the individual?

Physically, the body is flooded with adrenalin. This may be why a person throws up or goes into shock, cries hysterically or sits numbly still, staring into space. The person has to process the chemicals that have flooded the body as well as the shock wave of the event. A person may find himself or herself trembling for quite some time. Sometimes that shock wave continues to echo out for a considerable length of time, returning at the oddest times to 'haunt' the person, or cause them to relive the event over and over. Perhaps you could call it a stress wave. Some people will 'hit the deck' with a sudden loud noise, even 20 years after a traumatic event because their physical safety feels forever in jeopardy. Some people develop physical anomalies such as a nervous tic, a rash, a cough, headaches or changes in eating patterns, either extreme weight loss or weight gain.

## Emotional, Mental and Spiritual Responses

Emotionally, the person may find that they laugh inappropriately at what has happened. Some cry at the drop of a hat. Some withdraw and become sullen and do not communicate. Some simply want to sit still in a dark place, surrounded by safe walls and complete quiet. Others become angry and irritable, verbally lashing out over little things. For others, a peaceful night's sleep is an old memory. The less sleep, the less healing will take place and the greater the fear factor.

Mentally, the person is trying to wrap his or her brain around what happened. Sometimes things occur so suddenly that a person cannot figure out how to understand what just happened. They begin to search for answers. Often that search makes them even angrier, more depressed or more profoundly sad. Sometimes when all logic fails to get them to a complete understanding, they begin to lose faith in all that they knew, in all whom they knew and all that they thought they understood about themselves. In other words, they lose faith because the safety of the world that they knew is utterly shattered and they do not know how or if they will ever get that faith back.

What is also happening mentally is that the person who looks back at them in the mirror is a stranger. They no longer know themselves, who they are or how to function in the world. The world they used to know no longer exists and they cannot find their place, where or how they fit in, in this new reality. They want to be themselves again, but cannot find the path to that place they used to know or the person they used to be. They are now forever changed and they do not like this change. Sometimes they lose faith that they will ever feel normal again.

Spiritually, this loss of faith can be profound. The person may feel that the trust they thought existed in the safety of their loved ones, their family, or their home has been destroyed. The quest for answers very often takes them on a spiritual journey. That journey can help to take them out of their place of darkness into the light of hope and wisdom.

## Healing is Not One Size Fits All

We have established that one of the first issues after a traumatic event is the feeling that the person is not safe anymore. If this can happen so suddenly to a person leading a good life rather than to some bad guy, then the world is not a safe place! Security is one of the most basic instincts for all of us.

Once our emotional safety bubble is shattered, we do not know how to rebuild it. If the event occurred at night, there is a feeling that we will never feel safe again in the sleep state. We can heal all of this; we just have to realize that how each of us goes through the healing process is going to be utterly unique and not on anyone's specific time table.

We come into this mortal existence for the events of life. We are given the actual time and the physical space in which to experience life events. Sometimes we have a terrible time, a terrible experience. In the end, all that happens to us is just that: an experience. The person who ultimately finds his or her path to healing eventually has to come to understand this. How we choose to learn from the experience is what will spiritually heal us and ultimately define our spiritual path for many lifetimes to come.

Does everyone have the potential to heal after a terrible event? Yes and no. Everyone has a different emotional structure based on a myriad of factors. After the various holocausts that have occurred worldwide, it is astounding to see just how many people have achieved amazing levels of healing. However, our compassionate hearts need to understand that each experience of trauma and healing is going to be unique for each person and there are no simple answers.

Some people do not want to heal. They tell you they want to heal, but they wear the event like a martyr cloak around their shoulders, nursing the anger, pain, guilt and rage for the rest of their lives. These people are simply to be left alone.

Other people are so terribly damaged that they simply do not have what it takes to heal this trauma or any other life trauma. They lead a life as a very fragile person. Demanding that they heal or that they just "get over it" only serves to make matters worse. We can do the best that we can for these people, but we must be realistic in our assessment - there just may not be much emotional strength there to enable them to work our their trauma.

Some people heal to a certain degree and that is the best that they can do. It is wise to remember that the degree and level of trauma combined with the person's basic emotional structure will determine how much healing can take place.

Then there are those people who use the experience to grow as much as they can. They study it, learn about it, decide to do everything they can to make sure that it does not happen to someone else or they do something to educate people on prevention of such a situation. The bottom line is that they do something constructive. They use the insight of the experience not just for themselves, but they share it with others. They do service. Their service helps to heal themselves by helping them to regain their confidence, their emotional footing and, ultimately, their happiness. This is especially important if the trauma happened to a military person. That person is used to having an important mission and they need to re-establish their mission in life. Re-establishing this mission will help them to find a focus and a feeling of having a safer footing.

Healing PTSD requires that we make a conscious decision to realize that we are not all right. We need to accept outside help. If none is available, then we need to find someone who will at least listen and offer elements of wisdom in response. Sometimes we just need to talk about it until we are on the other side of the issue.

We also have to grieve the fact that we now know that the world is not necessarily safe. Anything can happen at any time. This will either make us a whole lot stronger or make us fearful for the rest of our lives. It ultimately goes back to choice: How will we use the experience? Will we grow, or retreat?

It has been said that the first freedom in all of life is courage. After a severe trauma, we have to find the courage to go forward with our lives. We have to be brave to heal. It takes courage to sleep at night if a tornado hit our home while we were sleeping. It takes a certain level of guts to get in a car after being in an accident. It takes courage to face life after a child dies suddenly. The more valor we can find within ourselves, the more we will heal and the more we will evolve as souls, spiritually.

The more courage we find, the more we will be able to continue loving others, life and, ultimately, ourselves. One of the slayers of many a good heart is the guilt and shame that many people feel for having survived a traumatic event where other people died. Everything that occurs happens in perfect order. People die. People die, very often, at a young age. We survive a terrible situation and others around us die. Why does it happen this way? This happens because each soul chooses the experiences that will help that soul advance spiritually. Some souls need the experience of dying in a situation and other souls need the experience of living through a situation. This is neither right or wrong, nor good or bad; it just is. We will all be released from a mortal body. What defines us will be how we lived in that body.

What ultimately heals PTSD? Allowing ourselves time to grieve, finding the courage to love more, even if we feel that our hearts will break with sadness. The more courage we show in expressing our feelings, and what we have learned from our experiences, the more we heal. That healing can come gradually in tiny, sometimes insignificant moments, or it can come in flashes of great insight.

After any traumatic event, we know for sure that we will never be the same again. That person we were has had a life-changing experience and the person we are becoming is not yet fully known to us. Accepting this situation takes tremendous bravery to see how each of us will evolve. Let that new person be courageous, loving, and dedicated to service. Let that new person be the bringer of light in the darkness of despair. The best healing comes when we learn to love who we have become because the traumatic experience made us stronger, wiser, and more loving rather than bitter, fearful and depressed.

Post Traumatic Stress Disorder is a temporary label. It does not have to define us for the rest of our lives. Let how we live on afterward define us as people who are courageously loving life and all the people in it.

## The Karmic Opportunity

The stronger we make our auric field the more readily we will be able to handle stress.

Traumatic stress causes us to lose confidence in the concept of living in a safe world.

We have to give ourselves time to process the energy and the lessons of the event.

We have to be patient with others and ourselves, as they feel the process of change begin.

It takes courage to heal trauma.

Ultimately, we are grieving what has happened to us and grief is a process of understanding the experience and healing the trauma of the event.

## Affirmation

I allow myself to grieve the trauma of this event.

I have the courage to heal the trauma of this situation.

I am embracing the tremendous learning experience of this traumatic event.

The Lightworker's Guide to

## Week 39   Lightning Bugs

When you live in the West, you enjoy the pleasure of low humidity, dynamic vistas, and glorious days of endless sunshine. However, when you live in the East, especially the Southern United States, there are some unique pleasures there as well, once you get past the mosquitoes, humidity and poison ivy. The Southern United States offers the jewels of gorgeous Technicolor countryside, the ozone producing summer drama of thunder, lightning and rain, and the cooling canopy effect of trees that grace every highway and neighborhood. But best of all, the South has lightning bugs.

Actually, without the rain, the heavy foliage and the powerful humidity, lightning bugs could not exist. For those out West or in other countries, perhaps it would be good to describe just exactly what a lightning bug is. A lightning bug is magic.

Lightning bugs, also known as fireflies, are little insects that come in at least two varieties in the Deep South, but globally there are over 2,000 species. One is a lovely light rusty brown and lives on leaves and climbs on plants during the day. When you can find them in daylight hours, they are still magical because they crawl on your fingers for quite a while before they extend their charming little wings and fly off a short distance to a nearby tree. The other kind is black with a red head. The larvae of lightning bugs are known as glowworms.

Fireflies can emit yellow, green, or pale red light. Their light is a cold light in that no ultraviolet or infrared rays are produced and 90% of the energy that they produce goes into the light, without creating heat. Contrast the efficiency of that bioluminescence to a man-made light bulb, which only converts 10% of energy into light and gives off heat.

Sometimes, even though you can scientifically identify what is happening with a creature, you may forget to consider how the existence of that creature affects you, that there is a karmic interaction between you. When you become an adult, you are often so busy being an adult, that you forget to remember what created magical moments in your life. You also forget to enjoy the wonderful things around you that are often subtle, gentle gifts of nature.

Lightning bugs start their mating ritual on sultry, Southern summer nights. They hang in the warm moist air at about four to seven feet off the ground. They are thinking carnal thoughts, so they forget to notice that they are easy to catch. Many a child has put a bunch of them in a jar with holes in the lid and hoped he or she could take the jar to bed to read by the light of fireflies. Little kids blinded by curiosity and innocence forget to notice that you cannot organize lightning bugs to glow at the same time. By morning, they are released and allowed to restore their energy for mating.

Sadly, fireflies light warm Southern nights less and less as habitat and pesticides destroy their way of life. However, near wooded areas where there are lots of trees and yes, also poison ivy, you can find them. These creatures invite you to slow down and enjoy those magical natural times where you can watch them living and being at one with nature. In those precious moments of discovery, you can be a little kid again and delight in those wonderful memories of childhood.

## The Karmic Opportunity

Take a moment and remember some of the wonderful things that nature has to offer and feel the gratitude that helps to keep these things in your life.

## Prayer

Heavenly Father, I send love and gratitude to the earth, to the sky and to the air for the life I am living. May I always be in harmony with the treasures of nature. Amen.

## Week 40 The Spiritual Path as Archeology

Dr. Sigmund Freud, the famed psychoanalyst, was a man fascinated by and a collector of all kinds of things, much like he collected the insights into the elements that defined the human mind. Freud gathered quite a collection of archeological objects because each of these relics of the past held a unique meaning to him. Perhaps to Dr. Freud, his own collections were a mere reminder that among all the 'emotional things' that define a person, you have to literally become an archaeologist to dig deep enough and sift through piles of seeming rubble to finally come to the truly hidden riches, the most valuable treasures of mind itself.

What then are the treasures of mind? What is the spiritual path of the archeology of the mind? Despite all the endless offers to quickly overcome your karma, or to immediately get past some ancient trauma or to just get over whatever it is that is bothering you, the truth is that over a lifetime you build up layers of emotions. You have to 'dig to discover' what is really down there, buried deep within you. And you have to be gentle about it. Like using a soft brush to carefully dust away the sands of time, you have to gently, carefully clear away the layers of emotional sediment that build up within each lifetime in order to move forward on your spiritual path.

In rocks, you can see the strata of the layers of sediment build up: water, erosion and the effects of weather. Everything leaves its mark on the land. In a person, you can also see these layers of pressured pain, or richness – like finding a vein of diamonds. Whether or not it is diamonds or coal, all of the forces of nature have an impact on the land. So it is with life, all the forces, all the events of multiple lifetimes create personality and eventually create emotional heritage. Some events make coal and some events make diamonds. All are carbon based; yet some can withstand great pressures and come out tremendously strong, brilliant and valuable. Others, however, emerge a little softer and find it harder to withstand certain life pressures – hence emotional issues are greater or lesser for each person.

You take these layers of emotions, experiences and traumas with you from lifetime to lifetime. In some lives, you resolve them and in some lives these emotional artifacts are actually created. Each emotional artifact will help define your spiritual path.

Today's flowerpot is tomorrow's archeological fractured find or critical puzzle piece. It is a question of condition: is it a potshard or is it completely intact? Often, yesterday's victim of being raped and pillaged is either today's victim, fearful personality, or strong crusader for justice/advocate for good causes. The person who was tossed out of a window by the Inquisition in Spain 400 years ago is probably not only still afraid of heights today, but may also not be much of a fan of the Catholic Church. That traumatic event and sudden death will mean that that soul's spiritual path will

# Everyday Karma

have been directly shaped by a past spiritual experience. You have to seek to heal that past experience before you can move forward spiritually.

Even if you do not know that you were tortured by the Inquisition, died in the crusades or were burned as a witch, you still have the opportunity to work through past fear to open new emotional and spiritual pathways. It is not necessary to access a past life to move forward in this life.

Each of us is a treasure trove of emotional archeological artifacts. One woman who always had a pain in her back discovered – through a careful return to the past - that she was stabbed to death in the Roman Coliseum. Another person might come to understand a total terror of trains by uncovering the long, tragic train ride to a Nazi death camp. Still another soul, who avoids churches, dogma and religion in general, may not have fared well at the Salem witch trials.

Along the way in your search to understand yourself by understanding your past, you inevitably come to appreciate the emotional structures that surrounded you, like the ruins of an old city. Those structures could be something as critical to you today, as food. Perhaps an old emotional relic would have been a life where you starved to death.

Many people come to appreciate an awareness of all the people from past lives. You find the emotional structures that either have always been there to support you or to hurt you. Part of the archaeology of the soul is learning why someone who so tortured you or so nurtured you in a past life is in your life again. Maybe that lesson was not learned. Maybe you are here to help them to heal, as much as they are here to help you to heal.

Finally, like physical archeology, it takes time to uncover a site. You do not just dig up a pot. You unearth a civilization, a society, and a way of life. You live it for a while and it lives within you. Eventually, you unearth all that you need to, then move on to the next site. This is why the archeology of mind will be eternally fascinating and hopeful. Sources of problems can be found, dusted off and healed.

Who is an emotional archaeologist? Sometimes that person can be a psychiatrist or a psychologist. Sometimes a particular emotional archeologist is not right for someone – maybe they were part of that person's past life and the match is not a good one. Sometimes the sensitivity required means that you have to find the rare spiritual practitioner who can actually take you deep into your past, especially if finding your spiritual past is what will ultimately take you into that necessary place of healing. Occasionally, you are your own spiritual or emotional archaeologist, searching your past to uncover the path to your future.

What is the role of the emotional archeologist? Perhaps this role is utterly unique and different for each person. We all have pasts that need to be gently uncovered, sometimes glued back together and healed. Finding a good emotional archeologist is worth the time and effort because you will be depending on their intuition on where to look for clues to the past. You will need their patience to gently dust away the sands of time. He or she will need to carefully, diligently and with a certain sense of leadership show you the way to living a life without having to haul around all the shards of prior centuries of experiences. While past experiences will always belong to you, they will no longer be hidden or pressing on the present. That is what makes it worth the time and effort to engage in the treasure hunt of emotional archeology.

At the end of a day, or the end of a lifetime, you come to realize that souls live forever, much like some elements of past civilizations. That lives of the past and the lives yet to be lived require a very, very, very skilled spiritualist to understand their connection. This spiritualist must gently, lovingly and wisely knit together all the elements which will ultimately result in physical, emotional and spiritual healing. Such is the real challenge of the spiritual path as archaeology.

## The Karmic Opportunity

Emotionally, we are like archeology, a collection of remnants of past lives, which are influencing us today.

By sifting through the events of the present and finding connecting events of the distant past, we can open a pathway for our spiritual progress.

We can heal our lives through the wise use of emotional archeology and the skill of a sage teacher to guide our way.

When we as students are ready, a teacher will appear to help us to heal and to grow.

## Prayer

Dear Lord, I pray for a teacher to show me the way out of the influences of past lives and present stumbling blocks. Guide me dear Lord, in the way of wisdom and light. Amen.

The Lightworker's Guide to

## Week 41  The Eyes of God

When God looks down from the Absolute, from the realms of Paradise, what is beheld? What does this Great One see?

What God sees is life's longing for expression.

God sees Creation in all its myriad forms in all of the realms of manifestation and fascination.

When God looks at each planet upon which life manifests, He sees beings embracing the experiences of mortal life, made possible by the concepts of time, space and gravity.

Without space there is no time and without time, there is no space. Without gravity, neither time nor space can exist. Without gravity, time and space, there is no mortal life or opportunity for experience, at all.

When God looks upon all the manifest forms of creation called mortal souls, what is seen are souls experiencing life in every way possible. Are these souls good or bad?

What is seen is neither good nor bad; it just is.

The sheer magnitude of life in all the realms, the seven Universes, the constellations, galaxies, and solar systems and on all the planets is the total realm of God and yet that realm is even more than this.

# Everyday Karma

We, as mortals, focus on just getting through each day and have a challenging time wrapping our brain around the sheer dynamic of the Mind of God. We do not realize that it is that very reaching out to touch, know and understand the Mind of God that connects us to this Great One. The more we seek, the more we are able to find, thus connecting us to the Mind of God in every way possible.

As we embark on this amazing journey through these experiences of living and dying, and the experiences of returning to Paradise or Heaven Worlds, we learn all the myriad ways that God has offered us to know the love and compassion of life itself. The more we can see our place in the Universe, the more we can be one with God.

What separates us from God? Perhaps what separates us is the fact that we keep separating others and ourselves from the concepts of God by not seeing life as God sees life. God sees the light and the dark sides of life as unique, wonderful, beautiful and as completely holy.

Man separates himself from God by compartmentalizing God. How can this be? What compartments do we create? We create artificial compartments in our understanding of God so that we can begin to comprehend what God is. These artificial compartments can be called tribes or groups. We belong to groups so that we can feel safe. This is primordial man banding together. Over time we give our groups names and empower them to represent us to God. Then we call these groups a religion, giving all of our power to these religious groups. We then start to believe that these groups have more power and connection to God as an artificially created entity than we could ever have as a unique soul. Eventually, every group will have a mortal soul at its head. This soul has no more connection to God than any individual, yet we falsely honor this specific person as having a direct link to God.

In the Eyes of God, we are all equal. No person, tribe, group or religion is ever going to be above another. We are all the same creation, with the same potentiality in the Eyes of God.

What defines each of us is where we stand on the soul evolution ladder. We create that level, no one else does. We create. We express. We evolve in the process of creating and expressing. In this process, we learn about love. We learn about what love is and is not and about God, even when we think we are going about that typical day.

We become 'God Like' when we can see ourselves as the same as another, removing ego from our concepts and judgment from our frame of reference. We become more in resonance with God when we can just observe the wonder of life's longing for expression and every person's process of evolution. Everyone is evolving at a different level in a different way and through a different process.

For some people, religion is an important step in that process of evolution, while, for others, religion it no longer important. Wherever a person is at this point is just that - where they are today. We can simply love them with all of our hearts. We can also love and be kind to ourselves. We can practice wisdom by releasing attachment to the outcome of any situation. This means that we allow a situation or event to play itself out. Sometimes we cannot control things and we have to have exquisite faith that all will work out as it is meant to be. We have to give up the concept of control in our desire to see another person, place or thing be what we think it should be.

Let things just evolve. Help in a positive way where possible. Perhaps that is the greatest gift each of us can offer - love without judgment or investment in the outcome. Perhaps when we can do this - even for a precious moment - we will come nearer to seeing the world through the Eyes of God.

## The Karmic Opportunity

In the Eyes of God, we are all equal.

In the Eyes of God, we are all souls evolving on our spiritual path.

In the Eyes of God, we are each uniquely loved, whether or not we are part of any particular faith or religion.

We emulate God when we can see other souls as the same as ourselves. We are each evolving in our own way, in our own time on our own unique path.

## Affirmation

I am loved and adored in the Eyes of God.

I help where I can and then I trust in the process of life itself.

The Lightworker's Guide to

## Week 42   The Spiritual Closet of Body and Soul

Did you ever notice that when people speak of themselves, they routinely separate body and soul? We have often heard people profess their love, their body and soul. However, did you ever notice that when someone dies, we always immediately separate body and soul from our discussion? Why is that? When we talk about the person in the afterlife who has died, we refer to them as a soul, we say that the soul has transitioned, or the soul has left the body. We are clear that we put a lifeless body in the ground but that the soul that animated the individual lives forever.

We separate body and soul on a subconscious and conscious level because they are integral to each other, but only when we experience mortal existence. Souls are eternal. Souls live forever. Souls come and go in and out of mortal existence. Bodies are like clothes we wear for certain occasions, certain experiences. We go into our spiritual closets and we pick the clothes/body we are going to wear to have a particular life experience. Isn't this fascinating?

In some lives, we will put on a military uniform and in some lives we will wear a fireman's cap or a judge's robes. Some lives we will be female and some lives we will wear a male body. In some lives we will have a large body and, in others, we may have a small body. In some lives we will wear a black body and some lives we will wear a yellow, white or red body.

Some bodies we choose because they have to last a very, very long time and some bodies literally last but a few precious moments. Whatever the length of mortal life, we chose it for the experience it offers for others and ourselves even if we leave as children or infants. Sometimes a lifetime for a soul is but a few hours to a few years. We do not always get to live 100 years of mortal life. Sometimes, it is but a brief sojourn.

If clothes make the man or woman, then so does the body. Some lives we are vertically challenged and some lives we have the perspective of great height. Some bodies are physically sick and some enjoy tremendous health. Some souls pick a body that they can learn how to heal. Some souls pick a body simply for the experience of abusing it.

Paupers and kings, computer moguls and maids all go to the same Divine "closet," pick out an "outfit body," pick up their spiritual contract and reincarnate.

Take a moment and picture yourself out in space observing this gorgeous blue planet. Come a bit closer and notice the astonishing variety of mortal garments from which we can each choose. Notice the amazing variety of locations we can choose to live!

Think about the volume of souls who are shedding their body/clothes daily. Roughly a million people die per day. Roughly a million souls transition out of a physical body and enter various aspects of non-mortal existence.

We are allowed to choose a religion to be born into and to experience all that entails. We are all born into a belief system of some sort. It is the aspect of deciding what we will believe that helps each soul to spiritually evolve.

This is important because our belief systems help determine our path. Some souls are born into a belief system and no matter what they are told, there is a non-stick aspect to them - they just never buy it. Perhaps they are wiser souls because they are able to touch into that sense of themselves that is God. Perhaps they are able to remember that we all go to the same Divine "closet" to pick out something to wear to experience each mortal life. Perhaps these souls know that we all come from God, that religion cannot separate us nor political philosophies define us.

Mortal experience is the most powerful and most concentrated opportunity any soul can have for soul evolution. The great texts tell us that in all of the Absolute, there is simply no substitute for mortal existence. All the spiritual beings that watch us work through our karmic paths patiently understand that we have to have the time and the space to work out the experiences that will enable us to grow spiritually. Even the most mundane, ordinary moment is pregnant with its consequence for spiritual growth. No energy in mortal life is ever wasted.

Perhaps some souls seek the perspective from outer space. We really are all the same, just a group of souls living mortal existence to gain experience, traveling on a beautiful blue planetary spacecraft acquiring the needed aspects for soul evolution.

Maybe the next time any of us uses the term 'body and soul,' we will look at the term just a bit differently, thinking about the Spiritual "closet" from which each of us have chosen to live. We are souls of the Divine, just dropping in for a bit of experience, now appropriately dressed for the task!

## The Karmic Opportunity

We come into mortal existence for the experience of it.

We choose whether or not to be male or female, to live a long or a short life and where in the world to live this mortal experience.

Ultimately, we are the same as everyone else on the planet, just dropping in from the heaven worlds for a bit of mortal experience.

## Affirmation

I have come to this life for experiences.

I am grateful for all the lessons from all the experiences that I have had in this life and in all of my past lives.

The Lightworker's Guide to

## Week 43  The Fuel of the Universe

What fuels the positive actions and events of the Universe? Did you ever wonder how it all works? Where does the energy of positive action come from and how exactly does it get to us?

Gratitude fuels the Universe.

Gratitude is the specific recycled energy that offers back to the Universe that which it sent to us.

The lofty things of the Universe are really quite simple. It is the essence of the Law of Attraction: what we send out to the Universe is exactly what is returned to us. The more positive energy we transmit, the more is returned. Perhaps it is just basic math, a very balanced equation of action and reaction.

Gratitude sent to the Universe, which is God, is an acknowledgement that the action was received and appreciated.

Appreciation is the symbol that our hearts understand that things are happening on another level on our behalf. Take prayer, for example. Lots and lots of people pray. Some people just pray for the spiritual practice of sending out loving energy to the Universe, asking nothing in return. They just do it because it makes them feel good. They do it in gratitude for the life they are living and the opportunity that they have to be of some level of service to people they do not even know. Is this gratitude?

Yes, actually, it is a form of saying thank you for the blessings we have received. It is also an acknowledgement of our growing spiritual awareness and the place where we are on our paths.

One of the most powerful forms of gratitude is the one we send for the experiences that we are having. We are thrilled to thank God for helping us to win the lottery, but we are not quite so delighted to say thank you for the horrible experiences we are given as well. The issue becomes one of seeking the specific lesson that every single experience gives us, even though they seem so terribly hard.

If we look for the lesson, no matter how hard it is we can really get to the other side of our anger and pain. It is these experiences that will enable us to grow spiritually. The more grateful we can be, the greater the pleasure will be of, hopefully, not having to repeat this lesson.

One of the aspects of true appreciation is getting to the place where we can cease judgment of a situation. As we rise in our evolution, we can hopefully get to the place where we do not label any situation as either good or bad. We are in a place where we can trust that this is happening for a reason and that, if we are patient, then everything really will work out well. Everything will work out for our greater good and we can look for the lesson. Once we have found the lesson, we can appreciate where it takes us and then express gratitude. That is spiritual progress on a sophisticated level.

Most people are polite and express gratitude through the please and thank you of day-to-day living.

This is the fuel that keeps the engines of progress rolling. It is the energy of ordinary courtesies that create civilized societies. We have come to expect it. These simple courtesies frequently make us smile and remind us that there are really some lovely people out there. These courtesies teach us to be patient with the process even if we are frustrated sometimes.

Parents teach courtesy to their children by being courteous to them, even the smallest toddler. What happens is that parents become busy, harried and stressed. Courtesy is the first casualty in how they relate to their children. Parents forget to be grateful to their children for the positive things that they do and then wonder why their children are not grateful to them for being good parents. The parent must provide the fuel for the family universe first to enable it to be returned and then to continue to keep refueling the entire family. Parents must remember to thank a child for calling if they are going to be late, asking permission, telling the truth or warning a parent about a situation. The more parents are grateful to their children for their wonderful behavior, the more wonderful behavior their children will demonstrate.

This same scenario goes for employers and employees. The more respect and gratitude an employer shows, the less turnover and illness the employer will see. The universe of a company is fed by the gratitude shown by management to employees as well as customers.

Gratitude is so critical that even the Internet is filled with the charming messages to one person or another about how special they are, how they helped a friend, changed someone's life or made someone's day.

It is always important to be grateful to the helpful people in our lives. Without helpful people there can be

Everyday Karma

no wealth. We truly need to help each other to get to that place of success. The more we are grateful for these people, the more successful we are.

We already knew that gratitude fueled the Universe. We just may not have focused on it before on this level. So tonight, perhaps it would be wonderful to slip into sleep with a grateful prayer to God for the fabulous opportunity of mortal life, all of its experiences and especially for all of the precious people, who so readily and courteously embrace us.

## The Karmic Opportunity

Gratitude sent to the Universe is an acknowledgement that the positive action was received and appreciated.

Be grateful every day for all of your experiences, even the profoundly hard ones.

Develop a spiritual practice of sending gratitude to God and to all of those helpful people in your life for the positive impact they are making.

## Prayer

Heavenly Father, thank you for all of the wonderful things in my life. Thank you for all of the helpful people who surround me every day. Thank you for my friends and family and for this wonderful body that I am enjoying in this life. I am truly grateful, Father, for all that I have, all that I have experienced and all that will come to me in the future. Amen.

The Lightworker's Guide to

## Week 44   Cooking Karma

Cooking is an element that affects every single person on the planet. We all have to eat. Whether or not you realize it, what you eat affects your whole life. Not just the presence or absence of nutrition in a fruit loop, but also the energy by which something is prepared.

Did you ever notice that some foods, such as a brownie mix made by strictly following the directions, will have a completely different taste depending on who makes the mix? With a brownie mix, you would have a reasonable expectation that each baked brownie mix will pretty much taste the same, but they simply don't. Why is this?

The spiritual frequency of the cook plays a critical role. Some food just tastes so good because the person cooking it has a great energy, which is transmitted to the food by the auric field of the cook. Some people have a different energy and the food - all from the same mix - will not taste the same. Even if you have two people with the same general energetic level, the mix will still have a different taste because of the unique differences in people's frequencies.

This is precisely why wives would be wise never to duplicate the specialties their husbands grew up with because they will never taste quite the same as what their mothers-in-law made. This is not because the wife is not a competent cook, but because no one can have the frequency of another and frequency directly affects taste.

How does this actually work and are there other aspects of this frequency theory? When you cook, you use your hands, and you use wood, glass and metal tools. Tools hold the energy of the user, especially metal, so if you make a cake and you are filled with love for the person for whom you are baking, then the cake will generally be delicious - because it is filled with the vibration of love. If you are irritated at a situation in which you have to bake, then you may find that the cake does not quite taste like you intended - adding to your irritation.

However, if you are really angry and completely resentful at something - it does not matter at what - at the time you prepare and bake the cake, the cake has the potential to taste just terrible. Even if it is not terrible, it will not be what people expected from you. You may also find that you burn yourself or the food in the process. Burns while cooking represent real anger within yourself.

It is also unwise to prepare food that you do not personally care for or have unpleasant memories about – you will definitely taste it in the food!

So, when you eat something it is always hoped that the cook had a good day and felt great when either he or she prepared the food. However, if he or she is not in the best mood, and you will not always know this, especially if you are eating out, it is a great idea to bless your food before you eat it. This is because prayer can transmute the negativity in the auric field of the food. See prayer below.

The karmic point here is that the higher a person raises their frequency, the greater the potential for creating great food. Negativity in food can literally make you sick. You imbue your food with your own frequency and you would be wise to give cooking your best. And if your best is going to be tired, angry or irritable, eat out!

## The Karmic Opportunity

Food takes on the frequency of the cook and that frequency directly affects the taste of the food.

Be conscious of your mood when you are cooking. If you are frustrated, angry or very sad, take a moment and rebalance yourself and your thinking.

Note the differences in how various people's food tastes and potentially why.

One of the critical lessons of a spiritual path is to understand how a person's frequency can affect everything, including things as mundane as food.

Bless your food to automatically raise its frequency before you eat it, especially when you dine outside your home.

## Affirmation

I love the people I cook for and the food I am cooking. I imbue all the food I prepare with love and light and energy.

## Prayer/Blessing

Dear Lord, please bless this food and fill it with the light of the Divine. Thank you, Father, for the food before me and bless the cook for preparing this wonderful meal. Amen.

## Week 45    The Resonance of Fear

What is resonance? Resonance is an aspect of frequency and harmony. The easiest example of resonance is music and color. If you listen to certain types of music, you become in resonance with that frequency of music. You become comfortable with certain types of music. While you can pretty easily go to higher and higher levels of frequency, you will find that it is much harder to go to lower levels of music frequency. For example if your frequency is rap or hip-hop music, you may have a hard time listening to opera or even classical. However, you can begin to change that resonance by beginning to listen to higher frequency music, even just elevator music will have a higher frequency. Eventually you can work up to the classics, such as Mozart or Bach. They are classics because their resonant frequencies are very high.

Color works the same way. If you are constantly in resonance with black, then you may find that it will be very hard for you to wear jewel tone colors or any color at all. Each color has a particular frequency. The more colors you wear, the more you are in resonance with a greater variety of color frequencies - and you may find that you are in harmony with energy at a higher level. Full spectrum lighting is full spectrum because it puts your environment in resonance with the full color spectrum of sunlight, which is a very high, very healing frequency.

Fear has a low frequency. The more fear you have, the lower your frequency. The more fear you feel, the more fear you are going to continue to feel. Fear feeds on fear; it perpetuates itself. This is why you attract what you fear the most because the more fear you have, the more fear you will attract. Literally, you become magnetic to it. The pull of a magnet is remarkable. Fear seems to have tremendous magnetic pull. A person who is beset by fears may find that they are literally fearful of everything. You may even notice their use of the word fear in much of their conversation on a consistent basis.

You also find this in people who worry about things constantly. If you ask them, they would not consider themselves fearful. They consider that they are caring because they are constantly worried about someone or something. However, the truth is that worry is fear with a caring face. Worrying never resolves things. Usually, it makes them worse because it attracts the very thing that the worrier fears the most. Then the worrier says, "See, I was worried about this and it came true." To that person, it means that they were correct to worry.

Fear exhausts us. This alone lowers frequency. It takes a lot of energy to be afraid. Fear is the ultimate diversion, a constant distraction. It is the fruitless maze of 'what ifs.'

Courage takes energy too, but a different kind of energy. Courage uses energy to lift you up out of the pit of fear and gives you the energy to move beyond that fear into emotional and/or physical safety. Courage is the freedom that enables you to grow. The purpose of fear is to give you the experiential opportunity to exercise courage. Courage is action in the face of fear. It is not action randomly. Fear and courage work hand in hand. The more courage you show, the less fear of anything you will have. Eventually you will not need that fear experience anymore because you will have learned the lesson, shown the courage. When you do not need an experience anymore, it just stops happening. This is a good test to see how your resonance has changed over time.

Fear lowers frequency while courage raises frequency. The greater the level of courage the higher is the person's frequency. This person is now in resonance with a different energy: confidence. This is courage that lives within you on a daily basis. This is belief in yourself because you have proven to yourself that you have what it takes to be courageous.

What's the worst that could happen? Examine the worst all the way through to the other side. Realize that no matter what happens, you will still be all right, you will still be able to live. What if it is death? What if you are facing death? The more you fear it, the more you attract it. Even if you die, you can come to realize that you merely transition into the next level. Release that fear. Shift that resonance to one of pure light.

Be a lighthouse in the storm of fear. There will always be fearful people. You do not have to be one of them. Release worry. Trust that, no matter what happens, things really will be all right. Trust is a courageous act. The action of releasing fear and embracing courage and trust, shift your entire karmic path up a notch. The subtle benefits will continue to echo back to you and you will find that you are a happier and healthier person.

Eventually, you will see that you are not attracting fearful, worried or angry people into your life. You will have positively shifted your resonance to a higher level and you will become magnetically attractive to higher frequency people as well. Such is the wonder of understanding the importance of resonance.

## The Karmic Opportunity

Fear breeds fear.

Worry is fear with a caring face.

What you fear the most you ultimately attract.

Courage lifts you up, enhances your frequency and improves your strength.

When you no longer need an experience, it ceases.

The goal of courage is to raise frequency so that you can cease being fearful.

Trust that all will work out well and understand that trust is a most courageous act.

## Affirmation

I have the courage it takes to face my fears and dispel them.

Courage lives within me because I am a confident person.

I give those I love my confidence in them, not my fear for them.

## Week 46    Karmic Time

What is karmic time? Perhaps karmic time is the sum total of time that we are offered to work out all of our karmic lessons as souls. Just how much time is this?

What did Christ mean when he referred to life everlasting? How much time is everlasting? Is this the concept of karmic time?

What does it mean when we say that someone is in his or her karmic moment?

As mortals, we like to think we have an understanding of certain definitions. We have defined our concepts and neatly placed them in little compartments in our minds. We think we have a generic understanding of time, but time defies understanding.

Time is the ultimate paradox. We talk about running out of time, or crunching time, of something being timeless or having a good or a bad time. Some people routinely speak of having so little time and yet, for other people, time stretches out endlessly before them. Is this all the same 'time?' Why is sixty seconds not the same for everyone? If a woman is experiencing terrible labor pains, every minute is an eternity. If an eight-year old boy is riding his bike, a minute of bike riding fun literally flies by. Are these sixty seconds the same? Are they the same if both events are happening at the same moment?

If we get into all the linear theories of time, what we find is that some concepts have time running in a neat and tidy straight line. Other ideas have time meandering through eternity in a slow and gentle river, and still other beliefs are that all time is happening at the same time. How can this be?

Time really is what we each perceive it to be. What is so amazing about time is that we can use it, manipulate it, stretch it and create it. We can also feel powerless in the face of time; feel that we are its victims and feel that time is cruel to us. Perhaps the best method of how to understand time is to go back to the concept of karmic time.

Karmic time is a critical facet of reincarnation. We return to the earth plane life after life to acquire all the requisite experiences necessary to participate in soul evolution. To evolve, we have to have time and space. We have to have the time and the physical space to work out all the karmic issues we create and earn life after life: the rich and the wonderful, the bad and the painful experiences. This concept of balancing the karma that we create life after life requires all types and lengths of time, actually, lengths of lifetimes.

What other types of time help us to balance karma? Cyclic time is the first. Cyclic time is the time of birth and death, day and night, and seasons. We depend tremendously on cyclic time to give us the security that the sun will, in fact, come up tomorrow and that no terrible day will last forever; that the bleakness of winter will surely turn into spring and that death will blessedly come when we are very old, so that we can try again during the rebirth time. Cyclic time offers us this framework, the very architectural grid of time. Cyclic time is the architecture of space in the cycles of time to enable us to have certain experiences. Cyclic time is the comfort of routine that defines our days, our nights and our lives. Plants and animals only live in cyclic time.

Linear time is measured time. We measure time in past, present and future time periods. We watch a clock. Before the invention of clocks, time was measured in days, months and years. With the invention of computers, we can now measure time in nanoseconds. This is perhaps why time seems to be speeding up. Linear time allows us to quantify our experiences so that we can put them in categories to remember them. Linear time is recorded by our subconscious. Karmic time is described in terms of linear moments. If we live in the moment then that karmic moment is in linear time.

Why is the concept of time in relation to space important? It is important because we can have a lot of people experiencing things in the same space, if they are separated by time. We can also have a lot of people together at the same time if they are separated by space. For example: Grand Central Station in New York sees roughly a million people a day pass through. So we have a million people in one space separated by time. We could not have them all there at once because there is not enough space. However, those million people are all in New York at the same time, separated by space. All these people are experiencing their karmic time at the same time separated by space. Everyone gets the same time and space opportunities; we just perceive and experience them differently.

Life everlasting is the concept that we are given an endless opportunity of karmic time and physical space, which occurs life after life to work out our tests, experiences, and precious moments. So no matter which lifetime we are living, every moment we live is framed in karmic space and time, whether it is cyclic or linear. How we use the space to experience time will determine what kind of time we will have in the next life or whether we evolve beyond any further need for time and space.

## The Karmic Opportunity

Karmic time is the time we need to work out the karma we create life after life.

We have to have the physical space and a length of time that stretches before us to balance all of our karmic requirements, life after life.

Cyclic time, linear time and karmic time are all happening to each of us at the same time but not in the same space.

## Affirmation

I always have plenty of time to work out my karmic mission and to enjoy the life I am living.

## Week 47   How Do You Love Under Stress?

How do you love under stress? The holidays are filled with need-to-do things and need-to-see people who all require your attention and love. So, how do you accommodate all of this and still keep your sanity?

The answer is multi-faceted. You can love under stress. You can behave in a loving manner under stress and you can take actions in a loving manner. All that is required is patience with yourself first.

Most of you who do service place yourself last on the list of people to receive assistance from anyone else. People who give are used to the feeling of giving and are not always comfortable being on the receiving end of assistance. However, people who are very giving need to analyze what they personally require, to be able to continue to give to other people.

Sometimes the emotional 'giving well' is empty. That seems to happen to a lot of people during holiday times. The reason the well becomes so empty is that the giving person seldom takes time to give to him or herself and frequently believes that somehow he or she has to be super human and get every last thing accomplished. This is not true, but you may believe that it is.

The Lightworker's Guide to

What do you need to keep the well filled? Here is a list. Every single item on this list is critically important to keep your personal well filled:

Get a great night's sleep. Interrupted, restless, useless sleep depletes the emotional well faster than any other thing. To get this sleep, you may have to get away even for a weekend to break the cycle of terrible nights. If you have to take something to sleep every night, you are treating a symptom, not answering a problem.

## Sleep Tips:

- Use ear plugs to have a more quiet night.
- Sleep in absolute darkness: use an eye mask if needed.
- Cover up or remove the TV because it acts like an 'eye' watching you.
- Keep your clock radio away from your head to reduce the electromagnetic field around your head.
- Play white noise if you live near a noisy area.
- Keep your room cool, around 66-68 degrees.
- Cover exercise equipment if you have it in your bedroom. Seeing it reminds you of work.
- Do not keep your home office in your bedroom: it means to your subconscious that your day is never done. If you have no other place for it, keep it cordoned off if at all possible with some type of screen.
- Use cool, calm paint colors. Red paint in a bedroom can be literally alarming for the subconscious and the subconscious is responsible for your good night's sleep, and body repair!

- Know when your day is ended. Your subconscious cannot sleep and cannot love when the emotional workday is never-ending. You will not sleep well if you work up to the very last minute and then expect to drop into bed and sleep. Give yourself a glide path to sleep by ceasing the workday 2 hours prior to the time you plan to sleep. If you cannot do that, then you have packed way too much into your day.
- Know what you cannot do and let someone else do it or simply do not do it. No one is outstanding at everything. Ask for help when you need it and let the person who helps you do their job.
- Recognize that you can delegate many tasks to your children and your spouse. Allow your husband or wife to help with the holiday gift and grocery shopping. You can delegate gift-wrapping and home decorating to other family members as well. If you find that this is a problem, you may have to ask yourself if you are way too controlling. Not everything has to be perfect. Imperfection is preferable to a stressed, anxious family. So the ornaments are clumped too much to one side. So the decorated cookies are a bit messy. Really, who cares? What matters is that you did things as a family, not that the family is artificially perfect. If your family is not used to you delegating to them, maybe you have held all the work too close to yourself. When delegating, elegantly dress your request in kindness and gratitude: "Would you please do this for me? Thank you so much! I know you will do a great job." These words smooth the way and

are much easier to swallow than "Do this or that because I say so!" Also, randomly mention to a spouse or child how much his or her help means to you. Again, the value of gratitude is beyond calculation and it balances the energy between each family member.

- Scale back expectations. Sometimes the amount of baking alone at holiday time can seem overwhelming. No one will think less of you if you buy a store bought cake or if you make something great from a mix. Not everything has to be made from scratch.
- Give yourself permission to give less, perhaps fewer gifts. Go to fewer events, have more nights of just being at home and actually enjoying the beauty of your decorated home, be it Christmas or Hanukkah, Thanksgiving or even just Halloween.
- Accept that another person may just have to be sad, unhappy or grieve during this time. Just because a Lightworker has a task does not mean that their presence or their work has to make the whole world safe, happy and perfect for all of humanity. You have to recognize that you cannot save everyone. You can be of service as long as you understand that other people have their experiences and that it is not up to you to preclude that person from ever feeling any pain. Love, but do not absorb the pain of another.
- Love with detached compassion. Love with all your heart but do not give your heart the pain of another. No heart can take that. Love, send prayer, send angels, send light and then detach. Once you have done all that you can do, your job

for the moment is done. This is especially true if you are experiencing your first holiday season after a death, divorce, or disaster. That first time of celebration is just going to be tough but you can get through it if you acknowledge that it will be tough. Despite this, you can still be happy. You can remind your family that you can still find pleasure in the season despite your loss. Your example will surely set the tone for everyone around you. Remember to smile as much as possible, even if you do not feel like smiling.

- Do not lament for what you cannot change. Some things just have to play out so that the person can have the experience all the way. Again, it is not up to the Lightworker to save everyone. That person quickly becomes a martyr and is not doing light work: control is the more operative word here. Never seek to control.
- Take time off for yourself. Go to the movies or take a day to enjoy working in the yard. Do something different. Be with people who consistently nourish you.
- Make sure that you receive physical affection. Give and receive hugs. Enjoying the pleasures of physical love will free the body of all kinds of pain and will remove great quantities of anger from the liver. It will also facilitate good sleep. Hold hands with someone with whom you feel close to emotionally. Feeling the warmth of a good person calms the heart and soothes the mind. If you have pets, spend extra time with them and allow them to do their job of calming you, of loving you no matter what.

- Visit a peaceful, calm place that represents a powerful connection to nature, such as a national park or places in the mountains, desert or ocean. Be in a location with different energy, one far away from where you live. If that is not possible, at least watch a happy movie or avoid the news/TV for a while to regroup.
- Contemplate your day. To do this, close your eyes and allow your thoughts to swirl around you and see what thoughts, ideas, worries or fears come to mind. Give yourself at least 30 minutes every now and then. Once you think you have identified something that is bothering you, decide to acknowledge it and figure out how to handle it. You cannot deal with an issue if you do not know you have it.
- Sometimes it is good to remember the purpose of the holiday or celebration. Go back to that symbolism of the holiday. Feel the love that it can engender. Feel the hope that a holiday inspires. Feel the happiness that you used to enjoy at the thought of someone's birthday or anniversary. Remember that feeling. Yes, things are busier, faster, and more stressful now, but if you think about it, you really do have more power over events in your life than you think.

The bottom line is that most Lightworkers know all of this already. None of this is new. The reality is that the information above is a reminder to be good to yourself because you are the example for others to follow. Not because you are better than someone else, but because you are conscious of your role and your job on other levels. Lightworkers have to be ready for the next thing that is coming, not worried about it. The service you perform while maintaining your personal balance will then balance the people around you. This is a critical element of loving under stress in these exceedingly challenging times.

## The Karmic Opportunity

You can love under stress if you focus on getting a good night's sleep, and allow yourself time at the end of the day to wind down.

Ask for and accept assistance with all that you are doing.

Allowing others to participate shares the workload and creates a feeling of teamwork.

Scale back expectations and allow things to be seemingly imperfect.

Understand that people may be extra sad at holiday times and that it is not your personal responsibility to always make that person happy.

Taking good care of yourself is a critical part of your job as a Lightworker and not something to be set aside.

## Affirmation

I love myself and I allow myself quiet, pleasant, nourishing moments with people I love and who always love me. I love the celebrations of life and all that they represent.

The Lightworker's Guide to

## Week 48   The Gift of Food is Love in Action

November and December are the months of food - scrumptious, delicious, gorgeous, fabulous food! Not just a little, but lots and lots of all types of amazing taste sensations. These are the months when we cook and bake things we do not make the rest of the year. We experiment with new recipes, try new foods, buy more than we think we should and spend a lot of time at the grocery store.

No matter what our spiritual belief is, be it Jewish, Christian, Moslem or Hindu, in these months in the Western world, food is among the many things at the forefront of our thoughts.

Frankly, food is one the most basic, elementary and precious gifts one person gives to another and this is an absolutely universal gift. All occasions are marked with food. In certain cultures only certain foods can be eaten at certain occasions. Some cultures fast - a denial of food - and then when they can eat again, it is not just a little food, it is a tremendous feast!

Food, at the most basic level, represents wealth and prosperity. In Feng Shui, one of the most important cures involves doubling the illusion of the cooking burners on a stove from the standard four to eight, using mirrors. The more burners, the more food can be prepared and shared and the greater symbols of wealth we can enjoy.

On of the ways that holidays (specifically Hanukah, Thanksgiving, Christmas, Easter and birthdays) are celebrated is through food. The use of special foods - foods that symbolize culture, tradition and family heritage - are prized and cherished. Recipes are handed down from one generation to the next, each cook placing his or her own variation on that theme. Thanksgiving is only about the bounty and blessing of food, family and friends.

Perhaps it is important to take just a brief moment and ponder how precious food is to us all. Food nourishes our bodies, providing the fuel to enable all the cells of the body to fire, our hearts to pump, our legs to move and our minds to function. Food is absolutely essential to our emotional wellbeing. That is why some foods - like macaroni and cheese, cheesecake and brownies - are just comfort foods. They may or may not be good for us, but, at some level, it doesn't really matter because those foods provide emotional nourishment beyond the physical. Good food feeds our soul, warms our hearts and offers us the very taste of love. Many of us well remember the aroma, the fragrance of fresh baked pies, the sugary taste of Christmas cake or the warm joy of Hanukah breads and cookies. Birthday cakes of all kinds are symbols of delight and a time when it is completely all right to honor ourselves.

As we plan our meals during the months of November and December, ponder our recipes, watch the cooking channel and imagine all those amazing foods coming out of our own kitchens, maybe we can realize that the real purpose of food is the service of giving.

When we cook, we give something of ourselves - not just when we shred our fingers grating cheese. When we cook, we put our hearts into thinking about the people we are serving. Consider the process of planning a birthday or Christmas dinner, as an example. Think about it: we talk to our families asking them what they love or what would they like. We try to make things that will please everyone. We consider making special things for each person because it means something. Of course we can also buy food for a person, which is also a wonderful gift to receive. Some foods from commercial houses are just delicious, especially if we cannot be there with the person to provide a home-cooked meal.

Back to our kitchen - we study our recipes, and plan the meals or party menu. We shop, mostly repeatedly because some things have to be purchased at the last minute. When we can, we bake ahead. We plan and plan some more. When we are actually doing the cooking, we are focused on producing the most delicious food possible. That positive focus is positive energy and we give the food we are preparing our own positive energy/frequency. We must always remember to refrain from cooking when we are angry, people will taste it on a subtle level. Literally, angry people create angry, icky food!

Perhaps we can put on happy music as we cook, maybe a friend or family member is helping us to cook and we are chatting and stirring and tasting. Our kitchen is warm, busy, and really messy and it smells great. This is love in action. We often give what we cook to others as a gift, such as a cake, pie, cookies, or soup for an ill neighbor. Cooking is the action of using our energy to create energy for another person out of the materials we have. We cannot just eat flour or spices. It is the combination of so many magical things that creates the miracle that is cooking!

So perhaps long ago, in the Middle East people also brought food to that manger to help that young couple with a new baby. Perhaps every time we share our food, we bring peace to our homes.

Let there be peace on Earth and let it begin in the kitchen, let it migrate to the dining room table and let happy hearts and friendly smiles warm our homes. So during the holiday season, as we all cook ourselves silly, we can smile because food represents love in action and that action is truly the gift of service.

## The Karmic Opportunity

Be sure to have a clear, happy, heart as you prepare your food gifts. People will taste the difference!

Encourage others to join you as you cook or prepare a meal: the shared experience at holiday time makes for wonderful memories.

Bless the food you make to enhance its frequency to benefit those receiving these gifts.

## Prayer

Dear Lord, please bless the foods I prepare for the goodness of all those who receive my nourishing gifts. Amen.

The Lightworker's Guide to

## Week 49   Giving and Receiving Gifts

Holidays very often seem vexing because of the requirement to provide gifts for people. Sometimes, the list of people to buy for seems awfully long. Why not simplify it so that you just wish everyone a happy holiday and be done with it? For that matter, you could simply wish everyone a happy birthday or a happy wedding or congratulations at the birth of a baby or a graduation or anniversary. What is the point of giving people gifts?

The point of giving people gifts is the very specific act of thinking and caring about them and pondering what would bring them happiness. The point of a gift is not merely giving a specific item; the point of the gift is to bring joy to another person. The only way to do that is to think about exactly what would bring joy and happiness to that person. That means that you have to get yourself out of the way.

What makes a great gift? The gift that the receiving person would love to have is the best gift. People often think of what they would like to have and give that to another person. Perhaps an example would be the sprinkler head repair parts kit that one husband gave to his wife so that she could always keep the sprinkler system repaired. Humorous as that gift was, it

# Everyday Karma

was actually a self-focused gift: that husband really wanted her to pay attention to the yard while he was at sea and he tried to make it easy for her. Ironically, this husband made up for the sprinkler head repair parts gift by buying his wife a six-carat Tanzanite from South Africa – something he was quite sure would bring her great delight.

So what do you do if you receive a gift that does leave you speechless because it is either ugly, awkward or not at all what you wanted? You smile, thank the person and consider that in their heart of hearts that person did put some level of thought into it. OK, the thought was not because they knew you as you would like to be known, but because they were at least thinking of you. Gratitude for any gift is important. What you do with the gift later is purely a personal, private matter.

The gift that the other person might really enjoy takes far more effort and requires that you think about the person with love and delight in your heart. It requires that you put thought and effort into it. Giving is giving no matter what the time of the year or the occasion. Any gift can be a great gift if the sender/giver believes that the other person will really love and appreciate it.

You may often think of the holidays or occasions as too commercial. Frequently, you may focus more on the hassle of the seasonal requirements and less about what you are actually doing for someone else. However, it would be wise to look at it another way. Consider that virtually everyone can remember a holiday or birthday when an amazing gift was received. Perhaps it was a bike, your mother's precious doll collection, a musical instrument or an intake manifold for a beloved project car. Perhaps it was a gift card that enabled you to have the delightful luxury of picking out exactly what you would love to have. Perhaps that gift card included lunch and a shopping trip with the giver of the gift. Now that gift is really memorable! If the gift is an art object or special ornament, every time you look at that item, you will remember the giver. You will smile at the memory and feel the generosity of the giver, thus feeling gratitude toward him or her.

Gift giving is work. It means that you have to spend time and money on many people. You have to budget your resources, your time and your focus. All of this reminds you of the importance of gift giving.

What about the person who seems to have everything? How do you balance giving that person anything when they seem to have so much? Give a gift of time. Time spent with someone can be more precious than jewels. Perhaps it is lunch and shopping or the movies. Sometimes it is a fishing trip, a ball game or camping. Sometimes the gift of time is giving another person attention, which they may actually crave. Often is it the intention behind the gift that is more important than the gift itself.

At times a gift seems insignificant because it is modest, yet the intention behind the giving may be beyond calculation. An interesting example of this is the donation of $1000 given to the San Diego Red Cross in December 2007 to help victims of the devastating 2007 San Diego fires. Two Camp Pendleton Marines on behalf of Col. Abbas Fadhil Abdul-Sahib, a Commander in the Iraqi Army, delivered it. Col Abbas collected the money from various Iraqi soldiers with the following accompanying letter: "We feel that we are connected with the American people. We will not forget the big assistance that the American government gave to the Iraqi people." (San Diego Union Tribune, December 19,

2007 pg, B2 "Iraqi soldiers contribute $1000 toward fire relief" -R.R.)

The United States is a wealthy nation; we literally have everything. However, that did not matter in this situation. What mattered was the intention behind this generous donation, which came at the holiday time. It was not a holiday gift, but a timeless token of gratitude and was an opportunity for a few Iraqi soldiers to give something back to the American people who have given life and limb to them. The magnitude of this gift may go unnoticed by some, but to others it is seen as a profound and amazing gesture. It is not just the magnitude of the offering; it is the magnitude of the intention. That is the real gift!

As you open any beautifully wrapped present during the holiday season you can honor the person who sent it to you and you can appreciate the wonderful intention behind it. Perhaps that will change your view of gift giving and receiving. The point of any holiday exchange is the love you put into your presents to others and the love with which they receive them. Perhaps that is the real reason for any gift-giving season.

## The Karmic Opportunity

The purpose of gift giving is the process of thinking wonderful thoughts about someone as you generously provide them with something they would truly enjoy.

The best present is the gift that the receiving person would love to have, not what you think they should have.

Ultimately it is the magnitude of the intention behind the gift that is the real treasure.

The Lightworker's Guide to

## Affirmation

I always think of the best gifts to give friends and family because I care so deeply about each of them!

## Week 50   Dropping into Drama

Before we are born, the family that conceived us was alive and living all the dramatic aspects of mortal life. When we were born, we literally dropped into the drama that was already their on-going life. Sometimes, we really complicated their lives and further intensified their drama. Perhaps our new life happened to them while they were making a lot of other plans that probably did not include us. In other situations our new family is just delighted to have us because we were part of the plans they were making.

Every single soul drops into someone else's drama. It is rather like walking into the middle of a play that has no beginning and no ending. We are born when karma says we are to be born, which is part of the Divine plan. None of us are 'accidents' although many of us are surprises to our parents. Karma always makes sure that we arrive at the correct karmic moment and that moment has absolutely nothing to do with convenience. Our parents, as parents have done throughout time, have to get ready for their new karmic bundle. Once we arrive, they may for a moment ponder what kind of a life their child will have, or they may never give it a thought. Some parents get this dreamy feeling regarding the circle of life.

However, most of the time parents do not think of those lofty things as they are just trying to get us to sleep through the night!

Once we arrive, we are immediately thrust onto their life stage. We quickly notice whether we have a sibling or a pet. We instantly notice whether our parents get along with and love each other or whether our arrival has created an angry drama. Sometimes the drama means that we are offered up for adoption so that another set of parents can show us the affection and care that the birth parents cannot show or give for whatever reason. Our being adopted is not good or bad; it is just another life play. That drama determination is very important to us because it will automatically define whether or not we feel secure in our lives.

How we view life will be defined by the first early moments of the stage play we have entered. As we continue to grow, we can tell how much each parent loves us. Some parents, however, are utterly incapable of showing affection. Some only pick us up when they have to and some literally smother us with their emotions. These early experiences of learning about how our parents care for us carve out our earliest lessons about feelings. We come here to learn all about love and sometimes we are offered the opportunity to learn what love isn't. This is as profound a lesson as learning what love is.

Many people feel cheated when they have a difficult parent. Perhaps they would be wise to view that parent as their most powerful teacher. That (parent) teacher will show what good parenting and family leadership are not. The challenge the child has is to separate themselves from that family drama long enough to decide to change it into a positive life. The wise and highly evolved soul will always analyze the drama of their family to see what worked really well and what was just terrible. Then, they can choose to change their own future for the better. However, the very slowly evolving soul sometimes repeats their parent's actions because it is the only thing that they know. They are often blind to their own actions. His or her blindness to the destructive power of a parent's tragic or toxic behavior is not because he or she is a bad person, but more because he or she has never seen a model of a functional family. Many people do not recognize the power of choosing to be different from their original family. That takes a lot of insight and willingness to change.

When we marry someone, we become an actor in that family's sitcom as well. When we start a job, we become a cast member in the office or job site soap opera. Think about joining the other theaters in life, such as buying a new house and entering the drama of an already established neighborhood. When we are hospitalized, we enter the drama of the hospital staff and that can be healing or deadly due to incompetence. We all know the stories of 'chatty' small towns and excessively friendly church groups, which often turn out to be just one concentrated soap opera after the other. When a new person enters some geographic locations, they are frequently, referred to as "that new person" for up to fifty years! People love their entrenched dramas. Imagine dropping into the tragic opera of any European royal family!

How we play our part in every stage we enter will determine our soul evolution, which will enable us to be wise or cause us to move backward.

Sometimes, it is a creative exercise to ponder all the dramas in which we play a role and then decide exactly what kind of a soul actor, we will be. In this exercise, we can also decide what kind of lessons we will learn and how we will choose to evolve as the dramatic souls we all are!

## The Karmic Opportunity

We all become actors in the stage play of our family's life when we are born.

Our birth immediately thrusts us into the drama of our parent's life and those early moments help us to define our relationship with our family for the rest of our lives together.

We learn about love and security from the way our parents care for us and that lesson will ultimately echo throughout our lives.

We have a choice in whether or not to emulate our family soap opera or to change that script for a happier life. We do not have to copy what our parents did if it was negative.

We spend lifetimes moving in and out of the theaters of our various lives. The key is to learn the lessons that these dramas offer.

## Affirmation

I am open to seeing the dramas in my life and to choosing to handle them with wisdom and intelligence.

I choose not to duplicate the negative, dysfunctional dramas of my family.

I choose to live a happier, less negatively dramatic life.

## Week 51   Christmas Time and Holiday Visits

The holiday program is about to run. No matter what your faith or belief system, all the glitter in western culture at this time of the year sparks lots of old memories and accelerates an upwelling of emotional 'stuff.' When you think about it, the feelings start with Thanksgiving and run through New Years.

During Christmas, there is a plethora of exciting, attention demanding colors, bright shiny objects, tons of twinkling lights, decorated packages, homes, stores, offices and entire cities. This Feng Shui effect of using bright, shiny things to stir up and circulate energy usually throws everyone off balance because it can be found everywhere you go. Remember the feeling when you finally take those decorations down? Whew! Things are so much calmer now! So, all those sparkly lights and bright decorations and root chakra (red) colors really awaken old memories and can accelerate your own personal issues. This is also why so many people feel extra tired and burdened this time of year – yes, there's lots to do, but even more than that, there is tremendous additional stimulating energy circulating everywhere you turn.

# The Lightworker's Guide to

Holiday time is beautiful, fun and exciting — what's the problem? No problem really, just an awareness of what is happening on a subtle level. This means that it is a good idea to be extra mindful of what is said or how something is heard. In your home, consider not decorating upper floors. Keep bedrooms undecorated and exceptionally calm. Everyone needs a calm sanctuary; make sure that you maintain those places in your home. Sometimes less really is better for emotional wellbeing.

It may be a good idea to be extra sensitive to your own needs as well as the emotional needs of close family and friends at this time. This may help a great deal. If a death occurred during this time of year, it may make the juxtaposition of all those happy people and your own personal sadness especially acute. If a divorce also happened at this time, again, some feelings may be a bit raw. This does not mean that you give up your holiday time. It means that you can acknowledge that which has made you sad or melancholy and yet you can still enjoy the season.

Which brings us to holiday visits where people are stressed. Travel less if you can. People are tired, stay in hotels if a relative is elderly and/or is not used to a house full of people. Shorten a visit or do not visit a person who is routinely pretty prickly and at this time of the year is a walking cactus. Sometimes, visiting can be a challenge because there is so much to do to prepare for a visit if you are the host, and conversely, so much to do to get ready to leave your home if you are traveling.

Traveling is challenging at non-holiday times. During the holidays, it can be downright nightmarish with packed or delayed flights and planes full of tired, cranky people! The other problem with traveling during this time is that, sometimes, you have to fly or drive to deal with a death, and/or a family or business crisis. Family difficulties do not always occur at convenient times.

Colds, flu and general malaise seem to hit people in December especially hard. These are old grief remnants, unspent or unreleased emotions manifesting in the physical body. Have extra rest. Have extra fun – go to the movies and enjoy yourself, or window shop for fun without having to buy something. Rest. Love one another.

What is happening karmically? Sometimes it is good to remember that December is the last month, meaning that all the emotions, hopes, fears, disappointments and triumphs are coming to a close. It means that, in addition to everything else, you have to take stock of the entire year. That alone can be quite challenging. However, it can also be a great opportunity to be very mindful of what is coming up for you, no matter what kind of year you have had. Remember the past with an eye for appreciating the experience, not grieving the event. Take a different look at what occurred so long ago and how different you are now – see how you have grown. Know that you are doing so much better on so many levels. As you go through the present, decide how you can make this month a wonderful time for yourself and those around you – which subtly changes karma in a positive way. Perhaps the best gift any of us can receive this year is the fact that day by day, in every way we really are getting better and better and better, no matter what has happened!

The Lightworker's Guide to

## The Karmic Opportunity

Be aware that the energy of bright, colorful objects, lights and decorations at the holiday time can be exhausting.

Refrain from decorating upper floors to maintain a peaceful haven for sleep.

Be extra sensitive to the feelings of others this time of year because old memories are always stirred with the energy of November and December.

Illnesses in December are frequently unspent grief. Address this grief and vow to have a wonderful, healthy holiday.

Travel less; do less, allow yourself to have a happy time despite the hectic nature of the month.

Review the year with an eye to improving your life in the coming year and vow to be a happier person.

Decide to say the affirmation below every single day in the New Year and watch your life change.

## Affirmation

Day by day, in every way, I am getting better and better and better.

## Week 52   The Birth of Christ

Why did such a powerful spiritual being as Jesus Christ come to live on Earth? There are those who would have us believe it was so that He could die on the cross for our sins and remind us for eons that we are awful sinners – that we are born sinners and that we will die sinners. Where is the hope in that concept?

What if that is simply not true? What if that was said to tarnish the purpose of the life of a Divine Master? What if He came so that we would be shown the lessons, the power and the purpose of love? Why didn't we know this already? Why weren't our ancestors living it already? The following theory might explain why He came.

Many eons ago there was believed to be a grand civilization called Lemuria located in the area of the Pacific Ocean. Its people were loving and caring, the new age we are currently hoping for they were already living. They also practiced quite a bit of spiritual magic. They were master manipulators of energy. Over time, they became more enamored with the power to manipulate energy than they were of learning how to spread loving energy and eventually their civilization fell. Remnants are still scattered all over the islands of Polynesia.

Well, these people had to reincarnate again, so Atlantis was started in the area of the Atlantic Ocean, and spread its civilization globally, incorporating lots of new people from other places. Again, a fantastic civilization was created. Its people started out believing in the One True God – they were the Children of the Law of One. They did well, following spiritual laws and creating a wonderful world. However, again, the manipulation of energies and the creation of power bases created a split among the people of Atlantis and a terrible darkness came and Atlantis fell – twice. Here, again, they did not learn the lesson of power, of not using the manipulation of magic for personal energetic gain.

The world fell into a terrible darkness for eons. Eventually, the souls of this time were allowed to return and created the instant civilizations of Greece, Rome and Egypt. Did you ever wonder why they just appeared? Did you ever wonder why the rest of the world remained barbaric but Greece, Rome and Egypt were amazing in their engineering/architectural and educational feats, some of which are unmatched to this day? The old Atlanteans and Lemurians were at it again. Only this time when they reincarnated, they were stripped of the bulk of their magic powers and ability to manipulate energy. Some people did have some memories of it, which is why the Bible is full of magical references, references where energy is 'magically' manipulated. Try using your average staff today to part the Red Sea – not too likely, but the 'staff' of Moses had remarkable powers, and the Red Sea was indeed parted. Moses did not abuse his power, but others in the Bible did.

People in ancient times suffered quite a bit, more than we probably can imagine. However, a group called the Essenes, were advised that a powerful Master would be coming to help with this suffering. They were told to prepare for his arrival, so they did. This is how they knew to look for the signs of the coming of Christ. They knew that there were many who would not want His coming to change the misery in the world and to give the known world hope.

So now is a good time to ponder the concept of what if the birth of the Christ was not about sin? What if the birth of the Christ was and still is about hope? What if we are really here to learn the lesson that the power of love, not power for the sake of power, is the answer? During his lifetime, Christ deliberately did not flaunt the use of magical powers. Christ's purpose was His message of love, not a demonstration of the power to manipulate energy. He used His love to heal people, but He could not heal every single soul because not every soul had the karma for Him to heal them. Do we doubt for a moment that He had the power to heal the entire planet? Of course He could, but He did not do that because He would not rob any soul of the power and richness of their karmic experiences.

The message of Christ's birth is that the power of love is the answer, not the magical manipulation of energy/power, not the guilt-ridden burden of dying on the cross for our sins. The power of love can heal the world. It takes great strength of character to live this truth. So as we honor the birth of Christ during the holiday season, let us also look within ourselves and find the power of our own strength of character to love more and with greater hope.

## The Karmic Opportunity

Perhaps the birth of Christ was to teach us lessons of love, not to create fear and guilt.

Past civilizations had the opportunity to embrace Christ concepts, but it appears that they may have abused the spiritual powers that were their birthright.

The lessons of Christ could be more about learning the lessons of the power of spiritual love and healing than perhaps anything else.

Christ taught us that the same God loves us all in the same way: there is no difference.

## Prayer

Heavenly Father, grant me the wisdom to see the world through the loving eyes of Jesus. Help me to follow His path of truth, love and compassion now and for all the days of my life. Amen.

## Bonus Week!  Mental Popcorn

Did you ever notice that when people get together and they begin to talk about ghosts, somehow everyone joins in? They join in with not only an opinion, but also with an actual experience of some kind? . . .sizzle. . .

Did you ever ponder why, when people are discussing religion, they frequently begin to discuss past lives and reincarnation? Pop!

When people discuss going on vacation or to a new country, more often than not, they will note how familiar the place felt, almost as if they had been there before? Pop, Pop!

Did you ever meet someone and note how instantly you disliked him or her or at the opposite end, felt immediately comfortable with him or her, almost - almost as if you have known this person before? Pop, Pop, Pop!

Have you ever taken part in a discussion about the pyramids in Egypt, the pyramids of Teotihuacán, the monuments of Tiahuanaco, or the amazing pyramids in China? Did the discussion continue to include Stonehenge, Angkor Wat, Chichin Itza, or Machu Picchu? Pop, Pop, Pop, Pop!

## The Lightworker's Guide to

Perhaps you and your friends gazed at the night sky and pondered the possibilities of life in Atlantis, or life on other planets, ancient and modern alien visitors? Did you then go around the group and ask if someone had actually seen a UFO or had a close encounter? They filled you with their delicious sense of either, dread, fear and/or excitement, didn't they! Pop, Pop, Pop, Pop, Pop!

Surely you have heard someone speak of a psychic premonition, a ghost story or weird synchronicity. This caused you to want to understand what this concept of what being psychic is all about. Pop, Pop, Pop, Pop, Pop, Pop, Pop, Pop, Pop, Pop!

Mental popcorn is created when even one person figures out that there is a staggeringly large world out there of fascinating, esoteric facts, opinions, legends and native stories to learn about that cannot be explained away by science! Pop, Pop, Pop, Pop, Pop, Pop, Pop, Pop, Pop, Pop, Pop, Pop, Pop, Pop, Pop!

These things are so interesting, so tantalizing that you begin to hunger for even more stories of the strange, the unexplainable, and the hauntingly tempting elements of the seemingly unknowable.

Yet, there are people who do know this information and how it works! These are the seemingly eccentric people who spend a very large part of their lives studying just these very topics. They are so utterly fascinating to talk to it is as if you did not realize how very hungry you were to understand this important yet esoteric side of life. These people will also help you to understand how to connect the psychic dots of understanding, the invisible lines of connection and the eternal historical threads that totally bind all of us together. They will skillfully weave the tapestry of understanding and, ultimately, help you to find wisdom.

These are the teachers among us who spend a lifetime in their own personal searches for truth beyond what modern science tells them is 'true.' These people will understand the esoteric and profound science of love, compassion, hate and viciousness and their places in our lives. These folks have an organized mind and they can delicately put the pieces together of why you hated your mother and how that may connect to a past life you may have had in, say, Brazil or China. They will guide you to seeing into the realms beyond physics into meta [beyond] physics.

If you are lucky enough to find one of these people, you will have entered the world of the disciple, the initiate in training, the world of the metaphysician. We can all enter this world - it is not for a few people alone. The only difference is that they long ago discovered the pleasures of mental popcorn and now fill out their spiritual diet with meatier topics and, often, healthier spiritual choices. You can enter this world with diligence, an open mind and an insatiable desire to know.

However, at the end of the day, at the end of a life, truly, the butter on that spiritual popcorn is the wisdom acquired by understanding, growth and the irresistible connection to the clear light of the Divine!

## The Karmic Opportunity

Translate your interest in the unexplainable into learning the real elements of the spiritual path

Your education earnestly begins when you can start to put the ancient, modern and esoteric puzzle pieces together that transcend mere curiosity.

Then you can enjoy the learning process of the world of knowledge beyond known physics: metaphysics.

## Affirmation

I am open to the world of the unknown through the diligent pursuit of knowledge.

The truest magic is the simplest act of love and compassion.

## Learn More About Tina and her Books

Tina Erwin, CDR, USN, Ret, has studied the spiritual side of life for many years, gaining insight into the interpersonal relationships at the heart of everyday living. Her writing comes from an intense desire to know and understand the unseen world of action and reaction combined with a sincere desire to share this understanding with other knowledge seekers.

Her lifelong studies into the esoteric side of life were further enhanced by the experiences of a dynamic 20-year career in the Navy, working for the U.S. Submarine Force, retiring at the commander level. CDR Erwin found the Navy to be a tremendous schoolhouse in which to study all the facets of human/spiritual behavior, from the worst, to the finest levels of humanity. She also noted that Submariners all seemed to have a heightened level of intuition, or gut feeling – truly an essential skill when you deliberately sink your ship!

Tina lives in San Diego, CA. She has been happily married to the love of her life, Submariner, CDR Troy J. Erwin, USN Ret for 38 years.

To learn more about Tina, visit **TinaErwin.com.** Here you will find many metaphysical resources, insightful YouTube videos and more.

www.ingramcontent.com/pod-product-compliance
Lightning Source LLC
Chambersburg PA
CBHW071303110426
42743CB00042B/1161